CHICAGO HOUSE MUSIC

CHICAGO HOUSE MUSIC

CULTURE AND COMMUNITY

MARGUERITE L. HARROLD

Belt Publishing

First Edition 2024
ISBN: 978-1-953368-73-7

Belt Publishing
6101 Penn Avenue, Suite 201, Pittsburgh PA 15206
www.beltpublishing.com

Book design by Jordan Koluch
Cover by David Wilson
Original cover image by Kevin L. Sanford

With love for Grandma Gert & Paw Paw.
Thank you for the music, and for teaching me how to ride the waves of sound.

For James L. Ballard & Jacqueline "Ki Ki" Williams.
Thank you for disco Saturday nights and Super Sunday passes. Rest in peace, my friends.

Acknowledgments

My most sincere gratitude to Andrew Peart for helping me find the initial spark for the essay that started it all and for continued support throughout this project.

Thank you to Eric Powell and Gerónimo Sarmiento Cruz, editors of *Chicago Review*, for publishing my original essay, "Growing up in Chicago House Music."

Thank you to Martha Bayne and Anne Trubek for believing in this project and for giving me the opportunity to tell these stories.

Thank you to my amazing editor, Michael Jauchen. It has been a pleasure working with you.

Thank you to my cousin, Kevin L. Sanford, for your photo that inspired the cover art.

A special thank you with love and respect to Darlene Jackson (Lady D), Kendall Lloyd, Czarina Mirani (Czboogie), Edgar Sinio (Artek/Cousin Edgar), Mario Smith, and Avery R. Young. Thank you for sharing your stories and for the love and generosity you've given the community throughout the years.

Love to Johnie Williams, Stacey Griffin, Joe Vergara, Jayh Johnson, Thomasina, Adrienne and Alicia Daniels, Danielle Gilliam, and Carol Fritzgearld. My Day Ones.

To the DJs who played the soundtracks to my life, Frankie Knuckles, Ron Hardy, Hula Malone, Maurice Joshua, Andre Hatchett, Tony Hatchett, Lori Branch, Honey Dijon, Derrick Carter, Mark Grant, Terry Hunter, Diz, Lil' Louis, Colette, Heather, Dayhota, Jesse de la Pena, John Simmons, Justin Long, Kaskade, K. Alexi, Ron Trent, all of the 3Degrees DJs, especially Jeremiah Seraphine and Julius, "the Mad Thinker," Duane Powell, Uncle Milty, Ron Carroll, Psycho-Bitch, Terri Bristol, DJ Sneak, Mark Farina, Gene Hunt, Gene Farris, Jesse Saunders, the Chosen Few, the Hot Mix 5, and Boo Williams.

To all the promoters, especially David Risqué, Rick Martinez, and Sean Alvarez.

Thank you to all the DJs, promoters, club owners, bartenders, door people, bathroom attendants, and, most of all, the party people who made Chicago house music what it is. Sorry if I left anyone out. You are in my heart.

For Chicago, thank you for birthing me and allowing me to carry you everywhere I go.

Table of Contents

Chicago House Music Timeline

1947 The first "discotheque," Whiskey à Go-Go, Paris, France

1954 The civil rights movement begins

1960 Women's movement reignited by the civil rights movement

1964 The Black Power Movement begins

1966 The Black Arts Movement begins

1969 Disco music is born in the US

Stonewall Uprising on June 28, the beginning of the gay rights movement

1970 David Mancuso opens "the Loft" on February 14 at his loft apartment in New York City

The Gallery opens, Nicky Siano, founder, DJ, and artistic director

Larry Levan and Frankie Knuckles begin their careers working lights, decorating, and DJing at the Continental Baths

The Paradise Garage opens

1971 *Soul Train* premiers in Chicago

1972 "Soul Makossa" by Manu Dibango released

1973 DJ Kool Herc and MC Coke Larock throw the first hip-hop party (the Bronx)

Grandmaster Flash invents the Quick Mix Theory (the Bronx)

1974 WPIX-FM New York premiers the first disco radio show

1976 The original Warehouse opens in Chicago

The punk movement begins in the UK

1977 Frankie Knuckles becomes musical/creative director of the original Warehouse

Studio 54 opens in New York City

Saturday Night Fever opens in movie theaters

Karen Lustgarten publishes *The Complete Guide to Disco Dancing*

The Chosen Few Disco Corp. founded

1978 Larry Levan becomes resident DJ at Paradise Garage (New York)

October Den One becomes Carol's Speakeasy, with Ron Hardy as the first resident DJ (Chicago)

WLS-FM Chicago becomes WDAI "Disco DAI" all-disco radio station

Technics SL-1200MK2 turntable released

Thank God It's Friday film premiers

1979 "Disco Demolition Night" on July 12 at Comiskey Park in Chicago

Executive Sweets / "Pat & Vera Parties," a "traveling club" for lesbian women of color begins

1980 New wave begins

Roland TR-808 drum machine released

1981 Frankie Knuckles sees a sign in the window of the South Side tavern called the Bitter End that reads, "We Play House Music," and Chicago house music is named

Disco declines in the mainstream

WBMX-FM Chicago's *The Saturday Night Live, Ain't No Jive Dance Party*, plays Warehouse-style on the radio, featuring "The Original Hot Mix 5"

Herb Kent's *Punk Out* radio show premiers

1982 Executive Sweets / "Pat & Vera Parties" reboots

Smartbar opens

1983 Frankie Knuckles opens his club, the Power Plant

The Music Box (Muzic Box) opens—resident DJ: Ron Hardy

Medusa's opens—resident DJs: Lil Louis, Armando, and DJ Rush.

1984 Jesse Saunders and Vince Lawrence of Z-Factor release "On and On"

1985 Roland TR-909 drum machine released

1986 Marshall Jefferson releases "Move Your Body" (the house music anthem)

1987 Jamie Principle and Frankie Knuckles release "Baby Wants to Ride"

Adonis releases "No Way Back"

J. M. Silk's "Jack Your Body" reaches number one on the pop charts

An ordinance passed by the city of Chicago goes into effect, forcing all-night juice bars to shut down at 2:00 a.m., the same time as most dance clubs serving alcohol

1989 Lil Louis's ten-minute "French Kiss" hits number one on the *Billboard* dance chart

House music becomes mainstream in the UK

1990 The Chosen Few DJs begin hosting the Chosen Few Picnic & Festival

Madonna releases the house single "Vogue"

1991 The city of Chicago proposes an ordinance that would require new juice bars to obtain special-use permits. They also require new establishments to provide parking for 10 percent of their customers and to be approved by the Zoning Board of Appeals. This ordinance effectively closes down all juice bars/ underage dance clubs.

1992 Ron Hardy dies at thirty-four years old

1997 The Silver Room opens (Wicker Park)

1998 Acid house hits the UK

1999 Moby successfully licenses all of the tracks from his album *Play* for commercial use

2002 The Annual Silver Room Sound System Block Party begins (Wicker Park)

2005 A stretch of South Jefferson Street is renamed Frankie Knuckles Way

Mayor Richard M. Daley officially declares August 25 "Frankie Knuckles Day"

House music officially becomes part of the city of Chicago's annual "Summer Dance" series, organized by Chicago's Department of Cultural Affairs

Mayor Daley proclaims August 10, 2005, to be "House Unity Day" in Chicago, which recognizes Chicago as the original home of house music and states that the music's original creators "were inspired by the love of their city, with the dream that someday their music would spread a message of peace and unity throughout the world"

2014 Frankie Knuckles dies at age fifty-nine

2015 "Move Your Body: The Evolution of House Music" exhibit premiers at the Chicago Cultural Center

Chicago House Music Conference & Festival, which includes panel discussions, educational sessions on Chicago house music history, and local DJ performances, is hosted by the Chicago Department of Cultural Affairs

The Silver Room moves to Hyde Park

2021 The Chicago House Music Experience, an interactive installation with photos, original party promotional flyers, and videos documenting the historical timeline of Chicago house music, sponsored by the Chicago Department of Cultural Affairs

City of Chicago Department of Cultural Affairs and Special Events (DCASE) highlights the locally created genre's contributions to modern music with "House City," a free, ten-part pop-up series that begins July 4. The pop-up events took place in Chicago neighborhoods such as South Shore and Englewood.

INTRODUCTION

Chicago house music is not a spectator sport. It is participatory. It is ecstatic in the way a Black Baptist or African Methodist Episcopal church service can be. The bass pops pieces of asphalt up off the street, and you feel the music before you even get to the door. The kick drum surges your heartbeat. The cymbals rustle the butterflies in your stomach. It's rapturous and the waves overtake you. It is the church choir, a juke joint on fire, a sonic tattoo. House music etches itself into your skin. Bodies ribbon together in the savory heat. Like church, Chicago house music was, and continues to be, a central force for social interaction, spiritual liberation, and community. For those of us who grew up in Chicago, house music is very personal. You'll hear the phrase, "Some call it house. We call it home," and in Chicago, that is the truth. To be called a "house head" is a badge of honor and a way to locate your own people.

The pioneers, the originators, the inventors, are Black. Gay. Chicago. While the genre has taken on many forms and traveled to many places around the world, it started in Chicago and was created by Black gay people. Period. I feel like I have to keep repeating that. So here is the remix.

Born in Chicago, house music is the granddaughter of gospel and soul, the daughter of disco and blues, the sister of jazz, funk, and new wave. Her children are techno, freestyle, jack, juke, trip-hop, EDM, trap, and all the others who claim her.

House music originated at the Warehouse circa 1977. It was created by Black people from the LGBTQI community. Combining city innovations, southern roots, and African heritage, it is a culture within a culture, yet it is not exclusionary. If you knew where the party was, you were welcomed in. Come as you are. Wear what you want. Be as you are or who you want to be. At a house music party, everyone is a freak and all the more precious for it. House music is what we want to be in the world and how we want the world to be.

Originally, house music was not necessarily about resisting or restructuring the dominant culture. It was about creating a space where Black gay men, women, and transgender folks could be free, safe, and expressive among themselves. It was a communal space, a safe haven in Chicago, which was often oppressive and repressive for gay and Black people. White gay culture was not accepting of Black gay men, women, or trans folks, despite a common otherness. Black LGBTQI folks were often required to present three forms of identification in order to gain entry into North Side white gay clubs. It was necessary for Black and Latinx LGBTQI folks to create spaces of their own. In doing so, they made spaces for all of us. The music quickly spread throughout Chicago, Detroit, New York, and London. Chicago house music traveled the world and came home to show us all the things she had in her bags.

Different from house music in the UK or New York, and the precursors to the rave scene, Chicago house music was not about drugs. The music is the drug itself, and in Chicago, it is the drug of choice. The feeling of music moving through you is the kind of euphoria people who do drugs are trying to get. There is an almost surrealist style to the way people move: legs kicking in the air, spinning, backbends, grinding, jacking, and jerking. There is someone with a tambourine, a whistle, a hand drum. To an outside observer, it may look ritualistic, tantric—these bodies, this communal art. The energy is so addictive. The release so complete.

If you listen to the lyrics in most house music songs, you'll see that they are about love and finding peace and freedom. They are about people finding their way out of stereotypical roles or bad relationships. It's about coming out—yes, sometimes out of the closet, but it involves more than sexuality or gender identification. It's about coming out from behind the walls society has built for us. Songs of triumph over the pain in the world. Songs of loss and grief and survival. Songs that truly represent the Black experience, the gay experience, the human experience.

House music is a place, a state of being, but it is not tied to any particular venue. A house party can pop off anyplace. It could be in any neighborhood in town, in the city or suburbs, in an underground black box room with only a strobe light and steam, a hotel ballroom, an abandoned warehouse, a beach, or near a car radio with seven teenagers dancing around it.

The party followed the DJ, no matter where it was. (We still call any house music function a "party.") Sometimes a club didn't even have a name, or it wasn't quite a club at all but a restaurant rented out on a slow night, turned into disco heaven.

House music is constantly in motion and ever changing. It is a dynamic art form. It does. It makes. It becomes. It takes hold of your insides and finds brightness. It finds your pain and brings you joy. It finds your weirdo and brings out your sassy, your funky, your truest you. There is freedom and liberation and hope in this music. Created out of marginalization and segregation, it continues to bring people of all walks of life together.

To say what house music is can never really be completely accurate, because house music means something unique to every person who experiences it. But once it takes hold of you, it will never let you go. And for that, I am truly grateful.

For me, this book is a very personal project. I wanted to write about Chicago house music culture and community and pay tribute to it. I write about the beauty, nuance, and diversity of my own people. Here, I have gathered parts of their stories, not as an observer or someone from outside the community but as a member of it.

This is a dedication. This is a declaration of love, gratitude, and peace.

My goal, as a native Chicagoan and someone who has grown up in house music culture, is to explore the music and the culture from its roots to the present day, and to highlight local community members, their experiences, and their contributions to the culture.

This book is for all those who make house music, who make the spaces possible, open, and welcoming: those places that were holes in the wall and places that had no walls at all. It is for the dancers, the disco bunnies, the fans, the participants, the promoters, for all of us who carried crates of records and for those who carry house music in our hearts. Most of all, this book is for Chicago. May she forever reign queen.

Chapter I

ROOTS AND ORIGINS

THE ERAS OF CHICAGO HOUSE MUSIC

Trying to write about Chicago house music in a linear fashion is a straight line crooked. It didn't happen that way. It is a complex mix of intimate circles. It developed as most communities develop, with different people in different neighborhoods, and in overlapping and sometimes opposing directions. The best I can do is work with time, which is also tricky. The 1970s, 1980s, and 1990s each had their unique aspects, events, and personalities that added to, changed, and shifted the various house music communities. Chicago's political landscape has also affected the way culture was expressed and, in some cases, repressed. Those shifts affected Black, Latinx, and immigrant communities dramatically and often divided us. But people in the house music community always found ways to overcome those divisions.

It took a long time for house music to become widely accepted by people outside the community. Even as it made it to mainstream radio, it was still only played on Black radio stations to largely Black and Latinx audiences. Some college radio stations, which have always been geared toward cutting-edge and underground music, would also feature house music. But once Chicago DJs moved to other parts of the country and started to play internationally, house began to gain more mainstream attention. But even then, many parts of Chicago still rejected house music and treated it as "other."

Another thing that helped house music gain attention within Chicago was the interest and influence of Europeans. In the early 1990s, several European documentaries highlighted house music originators, and a resurgence began in Chicago.

Even as the city government in Chicago has now formally embraced it and, in some ways, attempted to co-opt it, house music continues to be an underground community that takes on what each new generation brings to it.

Every era of house music has had its pioneers, creators, and innovators—those who have both nourished and carried on the traditions. Every era has also had a specific neighborhood or part of town where the culture of house music was shaped, fueled, and supported.

The first generation of Chicago house music can be dated between 1976 and 1983. During that time, early pioneers like Craig Cannon, Craig Loftis, Robert Williams, Ron Hardy, Frankie Knuckles, Pat McCombs, Vera Washington, Lori Branch, and Herb Kent began to play the music, promote the parties, and create the clubs and the atmospheres that eventually birthed house music and culture. The dancers, door people, bartenders, and artists all added to the mix that was mostly located on the city's South Side, primarily in the neighborhoods of Hyde Park, South Shore, and the South Loop. During this time, the term "house music" wasn't really used for the kind of music they were playing; people called it disco (and some of us still do). The sound was a unique blend of danceable R and B, funk, soul, Afro-beats, and disco. But the official term "house music" wasn't widely used, and it wouldn't be until about 1981, when people who frequented the Warehouse club started unofficially referring to the type of music played there as "house."

The second generation, and what I call the first group of "Originators," were most active between 1983 and 1986. This was only a three-year span, but a lot happened during this time. House music got its official name. The Warehouse, which is where house music got its name, closed. Frankie Knuckles opened his own club, the Power Plant. Ron Hardy's Music Box opened along with Medusa's, Smartbar, the Playground, and many other influential clubs. New clubs began to open all over the city. Many started to feature house music, or they at least had a house music night. The popularity of 102.7, WBMX's "Hot Mix 5" mixes every Saturday exposed a new, younger generation to the sound and the community. North Side neighborhoods like the Loop, Lincoln Park, Wrigleyville, Edgewater, and Rogers Park were becoming the central areas due to the location of the clubs. On the southwest side of town, Puerto Rican and Mexican communities like Humboldt Park, Little Village, and Pilsen were also making new sounds with high-energy grooves and Latin influences. The near south and west suburbs were also influential as tons of teens made their way into the city parties.

The third generation of Chicago house music—what I call the second-generation Originators—developed between 1986 and 1989. The Power Plant closed, and Frankie Knuckles moved to New York. Even after he left, his presence always seemed to be in Chicago in one form or another, and he came back frequently, especially for his annual birthday party, which was held at Smartbar. However, there was definitely a shift when he left. In some ways, the field became wide open for new DJs to make names for themselves. The availability of drum machines also meant people could make music in their houses. Chicago house music made its way to Europe. When Lil Louis's "French Kiss" hit number one on the

Billboard Dance Chart, house music officially no longer belonged only to Chicago.

The fourth generation, which I call "the Innovators," took place between 1989 and 2000. Ron Hardy, one of the most beloved DJs, one of the earliest pioneers of house music, and a Chicago legend, died in 1992, leaving a big hole in the hearts and minds of most of us. His death was more than an end of an era. In some ways, it felt like the bottom had dropped out from under all of us. Anything before 1991, or in Ron Hardy's style, was called "Old School/Skool House" by the purists. In the same way that we had "Frankie Chicago house music" and "After Frankie Chicago house music"—which refers to when Frankie Knuckles was in Chicago and after he left—we also had "Ron Hardy Chicago house music." And after Ron, well, it all became something else.

During this time, we had Derrick Carter, Uncle Milty, Ron Trent, Jesse De La Pena, the Diz, and Ron Carroll. We also had the influence of Detroit techno, including artists like Psycho-Bitch Val, Terri Bristol, and the ever-evolving Green Velvet (Cashmere).

The late eighties and nineties were all about the loft party. Like the early, pre-house days, the scene had largely been pushed back underground due to the juice bar ordinances Chicago enacted in 1987 and 1991, which basically forced all the underage clubs in the city to close down. Wicker Park, Logan Square, and the West and South Loop were areas that had large loft spaces, where DJ crews and promoters could throw parties for multicultural groups of young artists, writers, dancers, and house kids.

In the mid-nineties, partygoers were influenced by the rave craze in Europe and needed to find larger, more out-of-the-way places to host parties due to city crackdowns on illegal loft parties. Around the same time, hip-hop was also emerging and intersecting with house culture, and the near North Side neighborhood, Wicker Park, was at the center of it all.

From 2000 on, we've seen the fifth and sixth generations of house music culture—what I call "the Guardians of the Flame." In 2005, it seemed all of Chicago had finally accepted house music as one of the city's major artistic contributions. Mayor Richard J. Daley, with the support of then Illinois Senator Barack Obama, named a section of South Jefferson Street, near the location of the original Warehouse, "Frankie Knuckles Way." The mayor also declared August 10, 2005, "House Unity Day," with a proclamation recognizing Chicago as the original home of house music. When Frankie died in 2014, the whole city mourned and celebrated his life.

Today, the house community continues to flourish in the underground and in festivals that are celebrated all across Chicago, all summer long. Smartbar is still the most popular club, where you can hear house music Wednesday to Sunday nights, with DJs from all over the world. Just as house music has always articulated the emotions of its people, and just as it has always belonged to those seeking to make a way out of no way, this new generation of house music artists continues to create and push boundaries. And even as the current political climate tries to divide us, the house community will always be a place of love and acceptance.

TRACING LINEAGES: OUR MUSIC, OUR HOME

In Chicago, house music is more than just music. It's a culture, it's a community, it's a lifestyle, and it continues to grow and change with each generation. It is multifaceted and varied. It has a history and tradition, but it is also the "new new," which is made fresh with influences from all forms of musical expression. House music is part of our everyday lives. We listen in our bedrooms, in our cars, while doing dishes, changing diapers, and mowing the lawn. It livens up our celebrations, get togethers, family reunions, and parties—as they say, "Whenever two or three are gathered together..." And in Chicago, there will always be some house music playing somewhere. Listening to it, everything becomes musical: the distinctive whistle of the teakettle, the low bass of the steam, the tambourine jingling as the water bubbles inside the metal rises, the crackle of the fire underneath. The dog barking, car horns, sirens, and the click-clacking of heels on the sidewalk all seem to have a four-four beat and a groove.

House music is our hometown thing. You can think about it the same way you think about other things commonly associated with Chicago: pizza, Al Capone, Oprah, Michael Jordan, President Obama and the first lady, Michelle, the wind (or "the Hawk" as we call it). One way we survive blazing summers and almost inhumane winters, when the sky drops three feet of snow and the wind chill dips below negative thirty, is we warm up our bodies and our spirits with house music. It helps us make it through the week. There's also nothing like a "Hot Lunch Mix" to help us make it through traffic and on to the next thing.

It is in our blood the way country music runs through Nashville, like jazz and bounce burn through New Orleans, like go-go grooves in DC. We put everything into our house music like a sultry stew. You might hear some Bob Marley or some Third World mixed with some Curtis Mayfield, or Stevie Wonder mixed with our locals Cajmere & Dajae, Shaw Christopher, and Jamie Principle, next to some 808 State, Stone Roses, or Sneaker Pimps.

The thing is, almost anything can be a house song, because almost everything has gone into creating the house sound. DJs pulled from their grandparents' gospel and blues, from their aunties' jazz, bebop, R and B, soul, and funk, and from their older siblings' hip-hop, disco, Euro-disco, new wave, and rock. It was less about the origins and more about the groove and the vibe created through stringing together lyrical content, syncopated rhythms, and bodies in motion.

Our DJs like to tell a story, take you on an adventure, and help you ride your emotions to come out on the other side. Each song is not only about the beats per minute; it's a lyrical narrative where the melody is a character. It resonates and connects with your state of mind at that precise moment. It expresses that thing you didn't even know you felt. It shares some knowledge, reminds you of that thing your grandma used to say. It helps you understand what she was talking about. The way the DJ builds and links each chapter takes you to new heights and soothes your lows.

The DJ might start with Crystal Waters's "Gypsy Woman," which draws our attention to our unhoused sisters and brothers. There is the cautionary tale, as in Machine's "There but for the Grace of God," which warns us about how racism, homophobia, and repression can lead to the downfall of our youth. It could be Linda Clifford's "Runaway Love" or Roy Ayres's "Running Away," reflecting the lover who's been mean to you when you've been faithful and you just have to get away from them. Or, as in Diana Ross's "Love Hangover," it could be about the one you just can't leave, with love so good it's like a drug. Maybe you need to reconnect, and Odyssey's "Going Back to My Roots" moves you. Then the DJ takes you all the way back with Manu Dibango's "Soul Makossa," which is both a house and B-boy-B-girl, early hip-hop cut, directly from the motherland. Let the DJ put on Cajmere's "The Percolator," and the room is going to go crazy. There is a whole dance around that song, with body movements straight from the African continent. You might as well get out of the way and watch some amazing footwork, or do your own if you got it. Need to cool down but not ready to go home yet? Frankie Knuckles's "The Whistle Song" is the perfect refresher. The flow of a house music party in Chicago is a unique experience. It is communal art being created in the moment. What's made stays with you. There are songs that everybody knows and new songs introduced for the first time. Each community member has a central role to play.

The house music community really is a family—a very big family, but a family, nonetheless. Most people describe their first experience of a house party as something their cousin, "play cousin," uncle, or older sister took them to. For most of us, our first house experience took place when we were thirteen or fourteen. Lifelong friendships were made, people got married, formed businesses, and birthed artistic and political collaborations. Places like Literary Explosion, the Silver Room, and Beat Parlor in Wicker Park became cultural hubs that featured art, poetry, community workshops, and political action, all under the umbrella of house music.

The members of the house music community include, but are not limited to, the party people (people who go to the party, not people who "party," as in a euphemism for drug use), the dancers, and the general fans, who are lovingly known as "house heads." There are also promoters, crate kids, fashion icons, poets, writers, and artists. There are the venues, clubs, cultural centers, record stores, bookstores, taverns, and bars. The community also includes the staff, from the people working security to the people who take money at the door, to the bartenders and bathroom attendants. Of course, there are the DJs. But the most important member of the house music community is the music itself.

House also has its own unique fashion. Back in the late eighties and early nineties, there were people who would say, "I'm house" as a part of their identity. Back then, it was much more of a distinctive style than it is now. You can see some of its remnants within rave culture (though house never had that much neon), from the paisley, untucked, oversize dress shirts worn with a vest and a broach, to the wide-legged pants, bangle bracelets up to the elbows, and patent leather shoes so shiny you could do your makeup in them. There were also the preppies with pastel-colored Izod or Polo shirts, khakis, and K-Swiss. And there were the punk rockers (or punk-out kids, or punks) sporting Doc Martens, motorcycle or bomber jackets, spiked hair, and nose rings. Really, there was no other place in Chicago, other than a house music party, that had such a variety of fashion and where so many different types of (mostly) Black people would get together, at all. People come together with an understanding that there are some basic principles and rules of engagement. At a house party, people come in peace.

The basic principles of house music are simple: acceptance, love, peace, community unity, and freedom. These principles are born from a unifying energy, a shared necessity and desire to create spaces where Black, gay, young people can be safe. Where all people can escape the day-to-day grind and enjoy the company of friends, who become family. Developed by the community at a time when social justice movements, such as the women's movement, the gay liberation movement, the Black Power Movement, and the Black Arts Movement were all taking place, with Chicago as a central hub, the house music community was created and developed by people who were, if not directly involved, directly affected by one or all of these movements.

Nothing better illustrates the kind of violent, racist, and homophobic attitudes in Chicago (and around the country) than the infamous Disco Demolition Night. What happened was this: On July 12, 1979, a white rock DJ named Steve Dahl was pissed off because he lost his job due to the rock station changing its format to disco. He created an event where he invited the crowd to burn disco records and coined the slogan, "Disco Sucks." Not only did they burn disco records; they also burned other records by Black artists in the middle of Comiskey Park (now Guaranteed Rate Field). It eventually turned into a riot that made national and international news. While this incident did not birth Chicago house music, it did push disco, which was beginning to fade in pop and mainstream culture, further underground. It also brought Black, gay, and open-minded people closer together to form a community that is still thriving today.

THE ROOTS: PAN-AFRICAN TRADITIONAL MUSIC, SPIRITUALS, GOSPEL, AND THE BLUES

Chicago house music comes from traditional Pan-African songs, drumming, call-and-response, chants, and primarily West African vocalizations. It is this blending of the sounds from many different African cultures, sounds that the people who were kidnapped and enslaved in the Americas brought with them, that led to the development of Negro spirituals, work songs, gospel, the blues, and jazz, which led to all other forms of Black music, and maybe all popular music period.

In her book, *Black Feminist Thought: Knowledge, Consciousness, and the Politics of Empowerment*, Patricia Hill Collins writes:

> A common feature of African American work songs was the call and response format, where a leader would sing a verse or verses, and the others would respond with a chorus. This format came from African traditions of agricultural work songs and found its way into the spirituals that developed once Africans in bondage began to convert to Christianity, and from there to both gospel music and the blues. The call and response format showcases the ways in which work songs foster dialogue. The importance of dialogue is illuminated in many African American traditions (including blues and rap) and continues to the present day.

During slavery, dialogue among Black people was often restricted and, in some cases, forbidden. Negro spirituals, field hollers, and work songs often served as a way for Black people to communicate with one another in ways that the white overseers and plantation owners could not easily understand.

We call them "Negro spirituals" as a way to distinguish the sacred songs of Black folk from the hymns of southern white folk. It is a term of endearment and tribute paid to the ancestors and elders who used their voices to uplift and rejoice amid brutality, struggle, and strife.

Negro spirituals, like house music, are still staples in Chicago. We sing them in churches, at cultural events and gatherings, where we honor the past and commemorate our accomplishments, especially during Black History Month and on Juneteenth. As songs of gratitude, praise, and joy, the spirituals have always taught us lessons by showing us a brighter future and illustrating the dangers on the road when we stray from our path. During slavery, they were also used to literally help people find their way out of bondage and into "free states" up North. Spirituals highlight our full humanity by letting us sing out about how we all will, at one time or another, fall short. By singing together, we are reminded that everyone shares the same sorrows, that we can all overcome them to find the greatest reward in the end.

The belief in the promise of glory and an afterlife blessed with the light of the Lord was one way to deal with the cruel realities of daily life during slavery and the restrictive set of laws enacted after emancipation, otherwise known as "Jim Crow." Work songs and field hollers were another. These songs were used to keep up the pace of backbreaking work, keep the rhythm of the hammer, and pass the time, but they were also used to let Black people express their thoughts and feelings about the slave owners and the conditions under which enslaved people were forced to live, things that could get them beaten or killed if they said them out loud. Like the spirituals, work songs and field hollers also contained coded messages about the best times, places, and routes for escape.

Negro spirituals evolved into gospel music in the 1920s, and at the same time, field hollers and work songs became the blues. While gospel concerned itself with saving souls and the afterlife, the blues celebrated the joys of being alive and told tales about the woes of the here and now. The blues are filled with lovers done wrong, travel tales, and dancing with the devil and outdoing him. The blues reminds us that the devil is a man and that Jesus was too. It tells of our past troubles and capers we are currently plotting. It is like group therapy with drinking, cussing, flirting, and dancing. You can't do any of that in church, but you can let it all hang out in the juke joint or tavern.

Chicago poet laureate, musician, artist, and curator Avery R. Young describes the connection between gospel and blues as, "Mahalia Jackson upstairs and Millie Jackson downstairs in the basement. The same musicians that played on Saturday night at the juke joint played at church on Sunday morning." As a visual representation, he cites the scene from the movie *The Color Purple*, when the gospel choir is singing "God Is Trying to Tell You Something" on one side of the bayou, and the band is playing "Miss Celie's Blues" in the juke joint on the other side. Many blues songs and gospel songs are actually the same song, with different lyrics and slightly different tempos. But both blues and gospel are the music of the people, and they help express our deepest fears, our most severe pain, and our deepest desires for better, more prosperous lives.

House music provides the same kind of release and solace, the same collective, communal uplifting of the spirit found in blues and gospel. You can still find long-standing "Sunday Night Service" parties, where people dance until the sun comes up as part of their ritual. Blues and gospel sounds run deep in Chicago house music, particularly in women's vocals. Strong, dynamic artists like Loleatta Holloway, a native of Markham, Illinois (a Chicago suburb), who made the classics "Hit and Run" and "Love Sensation," illustrate the dramatic range and the emotional, melodic sentiment found in gospel and blues. Many Chicago house songs are literally gospel songs, such as "I Want to Thank You" by Alicia Myers and "I Get Lifted" by Barbara Tucker. "Jesus Can Work it Out" by Dr. Charles G. Hayes and the Cosmopolitan Church of Prayer Choir has been sampled in house music songs at least three times. The first was "Work It Out" by Karizma in 2017, then in "Dancing To" by Kurd Maverick in 2020, and most recently in 2022 in "Work It Out" by Bakermat.

JAZZ

Jazz, much like the Mississippi River, flows through nearly every musical genre, including house music. It was created during the mid-1700s in the city of New Orleans and came from the drumming and spiritual rituals of the enslaved Africans who met on Sundays in Congo Square, the center of the oldest African American neighborhood in the country, Tremè. The mixing of African, Caribbean, Italian, German, Latinx, and Indigenous cultures contributed to the sound and creation of the music. Like gospel and blues, jazz was influenced by work songs and field hollers. Early jazz musicians include Scott Joplin, Buddy Bolden, Ferdinand ("Jelly Roll Morton") LaMothe, Dolly Hutchison, Valaida Snow, Lil Hardin, and of course, Louis Armstrong.

One of the central elements of jazz is improvisation. Players riff in the moment, creating an inspired new sound through collaboration and interaction with the other musicians and the audience. Structured around call-and-response, the vocals and instruments "talk" back to one another. Improvisation is intertwined in almost every facet of Black culture, from the way we walk, to the way we talk, to the way we dance and interact with the world. One example is the Black Vernacular, otherwise known as African American Vernacular English (AAVE). AAVE is an improvisational way of communicating and expressing ourselves. House music and dancing are improvisational, communicative, and self-expressive as well. Call-and-response is expressed through movement and sound. The dancers call out and respond to the music, the DJ, and to one another. When someone yells out, "The roof, the roof, the roof is on fire," the audience automatically knows the response, and the DJ knows to lower the volume and sing along.

Jazz music is a staple in house music sets. You can often hear both the original version of "Sing, Sing, Sing," written in 1936 by Louis Prima, made famous by the Benny Goodman Orchestra, and the 1979 disco remix by the Charlie Calello Orchestra in the same set. "Cher Chez la Femme/Se Si Bon" by Dr. Buzzard's Original Savannah Band, which was heavily influenced by ragtime, an early form of jazz, is a classic house song and a fan favorite. Many dance songs remix and use samples from jazz artists such as Miles Davis, Mongo Santamaría, Lee Morgan, and especially Herbie Hancock. From the blaring of big brass ensembles to the small trio's snare, the sound and the free-flowing improvisational nature of jazz can be heard and felt throughout Chicago house music.

RHYTHM AND BLUES: OTHERWISE KNOWN AS ROCK AND ROLL

As Black people moved from the mostly rural South to urban areas like Chicago, Detroit, New York, Philadelphia, Los Angeles, and Oakland during the Great Migration (1910–1970), the music they brought with them took on new forms. Blues-infused gospel and gospel-infused blues were the popular music between 1940 and 1960. Radio stations featured gospel quintets, such as the Soul Stirrers, and artists like Sister Rosetta Tharpe (Rosetta Nubin), a gospel singer and evangelist whose dynamic stage presence, powerful vocals, and trailblazing electric guitar made her "the Mother of Rock and Roll." Artists Ruth Brown and Louis Jordan topped the *Billboard* charts. Radio stations called this music, which was the music of the Black community, "race music."

In 1947, the staff at *Billboard* magazine developed the category "Rhythm and Blues" to replace "Race Music." In 1951, a Cleveland radio DJ named Alan Freed used the term "rock and roll" for this kind of music because radio stations that catered to white-only audiences wanted a way to distinguish between white and Black musicians. (It is important to note that many blues songs used the term "rock and roll" in lyrics way before Alan Freed popularized it.) This was the Jim Crow era in both the North and the South, but the music knew no boundaries, and the young people listening to it were drawn to the groove. Ray Charles famously said, "Rock and Roll is the white version of R and B"—that is to say, rock and roll is Black music too.

Big Mama Thornton (Willie Mae Thornton) recorded "Hound Dog" in 1952. Elvis's famous cover was recorded in 1956. R and B was beginning to reach young, white audiences, and it soon "crossed over" to white radio stations. Many white musicians began making covers of Black songs, often without giving credit to the original creators. Sam Cooke, a former member of the Soul Stirrers Gospel Quintet, released "You Send Me" in 1957. He became a star, and it became a number one hit. The music of artists like Ray Charles, Little Richard, and James Brown all began to draw white audiences in addition to their Black fans. They played to segregated crowds all over the country, who were often divided by a velvet rope, not unlike the velvet ropes used to segregate the VIP areas of clubs today. But their love of the music often broke through that barrier, and people danced together, letting the music take them away. Police often arrested the musicians and their Black fans for "race mixing."

Beginning in the early 1930s, Alan Lomax, an American musician, folklorist, and ethnomusicologist, collected work songs from Black prisoners and blues songs from southern musicians, with his father, folklorist and collector John Lomax. He produced recordings, concerts, and radio shows in the US and in England that helped revive folk music in the 1940s, 1950s, and early 1960s. During the 1960s, British musicians like the Rolling Stones became fascinated with the blues and R and B and went to the American South to hunt down the musicians who created the music, many of whom had received little credit and even less money for their creations.

Much of early, pre-disco dance music was R and B. It was what was played in the taverns, bars, and parties in people's houses. Classic R and B artists like the Temptations, the Jackson 5, and Marvin Gaye influenced modern house DJs and house music tracks. R and B can still be heard in mixes and in the clubs. Modern R and B, hip-hop, and pop artists such as Beyoncé, Drake, and the Weeknd have all released new house-inspired tracks, paying tribute and helping the lineage come full circle.

SOUL

By the late 1960s, the civil rights movement was in full swing, and the music reflected Black people's fight for equal and fair treatment, desegregated schools, voting rights, fair housing, job opportunities, and fair pay. R and B moved closer to its gospel roots, incorporating the messages of the people, and soul was born. The music more directly addressed social issues and often served as inspiration and an anthem for the *movement.* In the 1970s, Chicago's own Staple Singers, "the First Family of Gospel," exemplified the blending of gospel, soul, and funky blues with messages of Black empowerment and civic awareness. They are best known for the songs "Respect Yourself," "I'll Take You There," and "Let's Do It Again."

Around this time, several independent record companies formed and produced songs that forever changed the shape of music and musical production. The four with the most lasting influence helped local musicians attract national and international audiences. They were Chess Records in Chicago, Stax Records in Memphis, Motown Records in Detroit, and Philadelphia International Records in Philly.

Chess Records started in 1950 in Chicago and was owned by two brothers, Leonard and Phil Chess, and Evelyn Aron. They focused mostly on blues and R and B, but they also produced soul, rock and roll, jazz, and comedy records. Their top acts included Howlin' Wolf, Muddy Waters, Chuck Berry, Etta James, Moms Mabley, Buddy Guy, Koko Taylor, and the Ramsey Louis Trio. They were located on South Cottage Grove, 2120 South Michigan, and 320 East Twenty-First Street. They closed their doors in 1975. The films *Cadillac Records* and *Who Do You Love?* are about Chess Records.

Stax Records focused on southern and Memphis soul. It was founded in Memphis in 1961 and remained open until 1975. Owned by the brother and sister team, Estelle Axton and Jim Stewart, its most famous artists were Otis Redding, Isaac Hayes, Wilson Pickett, and the Staple Singers. It was at Stax that the Staple Singers moved from singing gospel to soul.

Chess and Stax were known for their artists and the music they recorded and produced; Motown and Philadelphia International Records were known for their sound. Together, these two Black-owned record companies each produced their own unique brands distinct from one another. They created sounds that reflected the current cultural, social, and political climate in Black communities all across the country. Their sounds helped to shape, motivate, and uplift the people. They created the long-lasting legacies that make up most of what we know today as soul, R and B, disco, house, and hip-hop.

Black-owned Motown was started in Detroit 1960 by Berry Gordy, Smokey Robinson, Berry Gordy Sr., Raynoma Liles, and Gwen and Ann Gordy. Their focus was on soul and creating "the Motown Sound." Berry Gordy dubbed them "the Sound of Young America." Motown moved to Los Angeles in 1967, after the Watts riots, and branched out into film and television. Some of their most noted artists are the Jackson 5, Diana Ross and the Supremes, Marvin Gaye, Stevie Wonder, the Temptations, Smokey Robinson and the Miracles, Gladys Knight and the Pips, Rick James, and Teena Marie. Motown is still in existence and is owned by Universal Music Group, a Dutch-American multinational company headquartered in Santa Monica, California.

Philadelphia International Records was founded in 1971 by Kenny Gamble and Leon Huff, two Black musicians, writers, composers, and producers. Together, they have made more than 175 platinum and gold albums. They developed the label in order to rival Motown and their artists. Artists on the label included Harold Melvin & the Blue Notes, featuring Teddy Pendergrass, the O'Jays, Patti LaBelle, McFadden & Whitehead, Phyllis Hyman, and MFSB (the group that created the theme to *Soul Train*). Using elaborate bass lines, strings, orchestras, horns, and complex lyrical structures, with silky, high-register vocal arrangements and a healthy dose of funk, Gamble and Huff created "the Sound of Philadelphia," or Philly soul. Philly soul helped spark funk and disco and is one of the foundations of Chicago house music, particularly what we call "deep house." Songs with mellow grooves, large orchestration, and meaningful, uplifting lyrics that crossed the boundaries of musical categories. Songs like "Wake Up Everybody" by Harold Melvin & the Blue Notes, featuring Teddy Pendergrass, "You'll Never Find Another Love Like Mine" by Lou Rawls, remixed by Frankie Knuckles, and the famous disco anthem, "Love Is the Message" by MFSB. Philly soul helped usher in funk and disco with a distinguished sound that has stood the test of time.

THE FUNK

Out of the smooth, sultry grooves of soul came the funk. Some say that the *funk* has always been and will always be. James Brown is the undisputed godfather of soul, but he is also the father of funk. More than that, he is the essence of the funk. While he may not have invented the word, he certainly gave birth to the groove, "the One," and "the Funky Drummer" (Clyde Stubblefield). Listen to "Bodyheat" (which is, in my opinion, a masterpiece) or the opening bass line in Chaka Khan and Rufus's "Tell Me Something Good," and it will tell you all you need to know. Funk originated in the mid-sixties as a new fusion of soul, jazz, and R and B, with a "complex percussive groove," a drum and bass beat that emphasized "the One" (the downbeat with emphasis on the first beat of every measure—in other words, ONE, two, three, four . . .), and major, massive horn sections that were often the response to the singer's call. The most notable funk groups are James Brown and the JBs, Sly and the Family Stone (whose bassist, Larry Graham, invented the technique of "slapping" the bass); Parliament/Funkadelic; Earth, Wind & Fire; the Ohio Players; Slave; Lakeside; Heatwave; Tower of Power; BT Express; Zapp (Roger Troutman/Roger); Brass Construction; the Bar-Kays; and Rick James and the Stone City Band.

One of the earliest mentions of funk in music dates back to 1907 in a jazz song called "Funky." It's been written that Earl Palmer, a drummer from New Orleans, used the word "funky" to explain to the band how he wanted them to play: "Put some funk on it."

In a *Washington Post* article from 1979, "On the Difference between Funk and Disco," Geoffrey Himes provides a great explanation of funk music:

> Funk builds around a central dance beat that's slower, sexier, and more syncopated than disco. The musicians lock into that groove as if it were a hypnotic mantra but unlike disco players, funk musicians spin off dozens of sub-textures and counterpoint harmonies which orbit the main beat.

So much of the music that came out of Philadelphia International Records was funky that it is almost indistinguishable from regular soul. These were the sounds that Black people were listening to, that they played at house parties, rent parties, taverns, and clubs, all of the places that were forerunners to dance clubs and places that would eventually be called discos, and the music, some of the very same songs, would eventually be called house.

DISCO

Disco music is the mother of house music. Funk and soul are her fathers. Gospel, blues, rock, R and B, and jazz are her godparents. Hip-hop is her brother. Disco was at its height of popularity between 1969 and 1981. By 1971, nightclubs started moving the chairs and tables to make room for dancing. MFSB's "Love Is the Message," released in 1974, became one of the major theme songs of that era (MFSB stands for "Mother, Father, Sister, Brother"). The band is an orchestral collective of over thirty studio musicians produced by the creators of the Philly Sound, Gamble and Huff. MFSB was the studio and backup band for the O'Jays, Harold

Melvin and the Blue Notes, the Stylistics, and many other bands. They are the backbone of Philly soul and the lifeblood of Chicago house music.

In "Love Is the Message," you can hear the blended elements of jazz, blues, soul, and funk, along with the electronic keyboard, harmonic strings, and the "four on the floor," four-four beat that exemplifies the disco sound. The music evolved out of urban Black and Latinx dance parties, rent parties, and social clubs. Disco existed as an underground movement largely because the mainstream was not welcoming to Blacks, Latinx people, and other people of color. It was even less welcoming to the LGBTQI community. All of these groups had to create spaces where they could get together, dance, and listen to music without the fear of being harassed or arrested. Disco parties were taking place all around the country, but the genre of disco music really took hold in larger cities like New York, Philadelphia, Detroit, and Chicago, where there were greater populations of Blacks moving into the middle class. The civil rights movement helped to enact policy changes such as desegregation, women's rights, and affirmative action, all of which helped provide greater opportunities in education and employment for Black people. Middle-class Black folks had more money to spend and wanted places to go in order to relieve the stresses of the workweek. Many of the themes of disco music, such as relieving pressure, having a good time, and building up the community, made it feel like the soundtrack of people's lives.

Most dance music in the 1970s and early 1980s in Chicago was called disco, whether it was disco or not. The term "disco" became a catchall for any type of dance music. Even as disco began to decline and become more commercialized and parodied with songs like "Disco Duck," Black gay folks all over the country continued to party in clubs they called discos. Before the term "house music" was coined in the early 1980s, the music played at the Warehouse club, the place where house music got its name, was called disco.

You can hear the influence of disco throughout all of today's dance music, and it's also in hip-hop and pop. Artists like Doja Cat, Lady Gaga, Bruno Mars, Dua Lipa, Megan Thee Stallion, Chris Brown, and Drake all have current songs with disco tracks and samples. Disco never died, it just morphed into the *new new*. As future generations explore the roots of the music they listen to, disco's blending of genres will continue to shape dance and pop music for years to come.

JUKE JOINTS, RECORDS, AND TURNTABLES: THE EVOLUTION OF THE DANCE CLUB

Many of the first dance halls for Black people, particularly in the southern United States, were called juke joints. They were run-down shacks or old unused buildings that functioned as places where Black folks gathered—like a bar or tavern but much more rustic. Juke joints usually had music, dancing, gambling, drinking, and food. They catered to rural working people and began to emerge soon after slavery ended. Juke joints were one of the first safe and private spaces, other than church, where Blacks could gather away from white folks. Not to say that they were all peace and harmony; juke joints could be rough, but they were also community spaces where people could relax and be themselves.

In 1877, Thomas Edison invented the phonograph. Emile Berliner invented the gramophone record ten years later, and the first jukebox was invented by Louis Glass two years after that. They became popular during the Great Depression, when most people couldn't afford to hire a band or buy records.

During World War II, when the Germans occupied France, the Nazis banned American music like jazz, swing, and bebop, and dances like the Lindy Hop and the Jitterbug, seeing them as "decadent"

American influences. As an act of rebellion, people met in hidden basements and clandestine speakeasies, where they danced to the jazz and swing that was played on a single turntable when a jukebox was not available. They called these places "discothèques," which literally means "library of phonographic records." The word "disco" is a shortened version of that.

The first discothèque, Le Whisky à Gogo, was founded in Paris in 1947 by Régine Zylberberg. In 1953, she laid a dance floor, strung colored lights, and replaced the jukebox with two turntables, which she operated herself, so the music could play continuously. She recalled in an interview with BBC News UK, "Instead I installed two turntables so there was no gap in the music. I was barmaid, doorman, bathroom attendant, hostess—and I also put on the records. It was the first ever discotheque and I was the first ever club disc-jockey."

JIM CROW, SEGREGATION, AND STONEWALL

Régine Zylberberg was a pioneer for being a woman business owner and for her revolutionary techniques as a DJ. Meanwhile, in all of the emerging dance scenes in the US, the pioneers were Black, Latinx, and LGBTQI people. They were partying, celebrating their lives, and getting down to the music in their own taverns, juke joints, bars, speakeasies, rent parties, and crowded basements. They had fabulous, sometimes lush decor, with colored party lights, balloons, and streamers. Sometimes they had little more than the music and each other. They made spaces for themselves. They made due, partly because they wanted and needed spaces where they could be with their communities and partly because, often, they were not legally allowed to gather anywhere else. "Race mixing"—interracial marriage, dating, and cohabitation—was illegal in most states until 1967.

Even being at a party with a person of a different race could land someone in jail or worse.

During this era, there were significant African American populations in all northern cities, and during the Great Migration, the numbers of African Americans increased significantly. People came up from the South, seeking better jobs, higher wages, better living conditions, and more civil liberties. Many found employment opportunities and better wages, but they also found that Jim Crow was alive and well in the North (or "Up South" as some called it). Racism, segregation, and discrimination, while not always as overt as it was in the South, but still kept Black people from achieving equality, often in more insidious and far-reaching ways.

The most famous example of this was redlining, which restricted the places where Black, Latinx, and other ethnic minorities could live. Government officials literally drew red lines on maps indicating those areas. They enacted federal policies that classified Black, Latinx, and low-income neighborhoods as "hazardous" or "undesirable" for investment, credit, mortgages, insurance, and services, which led to further racial segregation, urban decay, predatory lending, and inequalities in housing and education. The Fair Housing Act was passed in 1968, though the practice of redlining continues today under the name of "urban renewal" or "gentrification," particularly in cities like Chicago, Detroit, Washington, DC, Philadelphia, Atlanta, and New York.

For the LGBTQI community, times were also tough. For Black and Latinx LGBTQI folks, it was even worse. Before 1962, sodomy was considered a felony in every state, punishable by long prison terms and/or hard labor. In 1962, Illinois became the first state to remove criminal penalties for consensual sodomy from its criminal code. That did not necessarily stop the harassment from both police and private citizens, however.

Sodomy laws and cabaret ordinances made it illegal for people in LGBTQI communities to show any kind of public affection with one another, such as holding hands and dancing with someone of the same gender. Asking someone of the same gender out on a date was considered "solicitation" and was also illegal. State and local liquor licensing boards would shut down establishments known or suspected of catering to LGBTQI clients. Many places operated underground and without liquor licenses. Much like in Black and Latinx communities, any gathering of LGBTQI people was considered "disorderly" and was frequently subjected to police harassment.

The Stonewall Inn was an LGBTQI bar in the Greenwich Village neighborhood in New York City. It operated as a private "bottle bar," where clients brought their own liquor as a way to skirt the city's liquor license ordinance. It was owned by the mafia, like many gay bars and clubs in New York at the time. They offered some protection to patrons by paying off police, but they also blackmailed some of the wealthier customers, threatening to "out" them. Stonewall was well-known as a refuge in New York, particularly for unhoused youth and transgender people, who were often discriminated against at other gay bars.

On the night of June 28, 1969, the police entered the club with a warrant, targeting the bar for operating without a liquor license. There were eight undercover police officers who singled out transgender patrons, taking them in the bathroom to "check" to see if they were "real" women; in New York at the time, "masquerading" as a member of the opposite gender was illegal. They arrested thirteen people, many of whom were African American trans women. They physically assaulted and rough-handled employees and patrons. Customers and neighborhood residents, fed up with the discrimination, harassment, and brutality, gathered around the bar and resisted. Police beat and tear-gassed members of the crowd, and an uprising began that lasted six days. Despite being torn up by police, the Stonewall Inn became a gathering place for LGBTQI activists and their allies. A year later, they launched the Christopher Street Liberation March, which became New York's first Gay Pride Parade.

The history of the Stonewall Uprising is an important example of how difficult it was for marginalized groups around the country to gather and dance in peace. It is important as an illustration of how a bar or dance club can help build community and be a safe space. The house music community would become a central part of that in Chicago. Though the Stonewall Uprising did not start the gay rights movement, it acted as a catalyst for LGBTQI rights movements around the world.

Even in places that were created by LGBTQI folks as safe spaces, they were not always welcoming or safe spaces for Black, Latinx, and other marginalized communities. Establishments that catered to gay men were not always welcoming to lesbians or transgender people, for example. Even in the midst of the gay rights movement, the women's liberation movement, the Black Power Movement, and the civil rights movement, people within these groups, and the places they frequented, had their own brands of exclusivity, discrimination, sexism, and racism. One of the things disco did was help to bring all different kinds of people together in spaces where they could be exposed to those they otherwise would not have associated with or had access to.

In the early 1970s, dance culture in the Black, Latinx, and LGBTQI communities was filled with the ideals of peace and love that came out of the cultural revolutions and community activism of the 1960s, and it blended with the rage, disillusionment, new ideals, and radical funk that emerged in the 1970s. It was about inclusion, community building, and the liberation of the mind, body, and spirit. The discos and nightclubs themselves were revolutionary simply because they existed despite laws, ordinances, and prejudices that were designed to marginalize them.

People wanted to be free, and dancing became a way for them to express those freedoms.

LADIES IN THE HOUSE

The origins of house music have their direct lineage in the Black gay clubs on the South and West Sides of Chicago, and while the men get most of the credit, women were in those clubs too. They were DJs, promoters, business partners, patrons, and community members who provided integral support. Women threw their own parties, helped fund other people's parties, worked the door (David Risqué's mom worked the door at Sauer's, and Robert Williams's mom worked at the Warehouse). They prepared food, played the music, and most of all, gave their voices to the songs we were all dancing to. Without the women, there would be no house music in Chicago or anywhere else. Every other form of music that includes vocals would be less sweet.

Nearly all the songs that have meaning, the songs where we know every single word and sing out loud as if our lives depended on it, all the songs that have the kind of emotional heights and depths that bring us to tears, that take us so profoundly within ourselves that we surrender—almost every one of those songs has powerful, commanding, soulful female vocals. Now don't get me wrong, Teddy Pendergrass's deep, throaty begging, and the sultry conga followed by the sweet strings in the intro to "Don't Leave Me This Way" does a little something special for me. But Thelma Houston's version is the jam that takes over my whole body. Her silky, virtually angelic voice, that bass, the high hat, and that funky groove in the chorus, especially when the tambourine breaks in, take me to church and beyond.

The heavy gospel and jazz influences that give their voices such range and intensity can be heard in early legendary disco divas like Donna Summer, Diana Ross, Martha Wash, Sister Sledge, Sylvester, and our hometown heroine, Loleatta Holloway (especially in "Hit and Run" and "Love Sensation"). We experience the soulful Latin and Caribbean undertones in classic singers like Vicki Sue Robinson ("Turn the Beat Around"), Clare Bathé, from the band Machine ("There but for the Grace of God"), Lillian Lopez from Odyssey ("Native New Yorker" and "Inside Out"), and Cory Daye from Dr. Buzzard's Original Savannah Band ("Cherchez la Femme"). The nineties produced another local favorite, Shawn Christopher, whose music made the charts as a solo artist ("Another Sleepless Night") and as a singer with the electronic/industrial rock band My Life with the Thrill Kill Kult. Other classic female hitmakers included British vocalists Doreen Waddell, Caron Wheeler, and Rose Windross from Soul II Soul ("Back to Life (However Do You Want Me)" and "Keep On Movin'"), Robin S. ("Show Me Love"), Lady Miss Kier from Deee-Lite ("Groove Is in the Heart"), Ultra Naté ("Free"), and the beloved Crystal Waters ("Gypsy Woman," "100% Pure Love"). And while she doesn't possess the characteristically soulful, harmonic voice of many other female vocalists, Miss Grace Jones is in a class all by herself, having been one of the first to bridge the music, art, and fashion worlds. She is a trendsetter and the ultimate example of unbridled freedom.

Chapter 2

THE PIONEERS, 1970–1975

DAVID MANCUSO'S LOFT AND *SOUL TRAIN*

While disco was beginning to bloom underground in various cities, the parties at David Mancuso's Loft in New York pioneered what was to become the modern disco and dance music club scene. Mancuso was an antique dealer who started throwing rent parties at his downtown loft in 1965. These were private events, but they were not exclusive; people who attended could bring a friend or two. The crowd was an ethnically and economically diverse group of mostly young, gay, Black, Latinx, and white folks, along with artists and other freethinking people. On Valentine's Day in 1970, Mancuso threw a themed party that was so successful he decided to do it every week. In a 2007 interview with Tim Lawrence at *Red Bull Music Academy*, he discussed his gatherings and how they were different than nightclubs:

> Clubs are set up for the purpose of making money. This is not what The Loft is about. The Loft is about putting on a party and making

> friends. That doesn't mean you can't put on a party and make friends in a club, but these places are structured to make a profit, and that's a whole different head. Without a doubt, that has a bearing on how things happen and how far things can go. For me The Loft is all about social progress. With my own parties you can bring your own alcohol and your children can come along. If I couldn't find a location where these things could happen I'd be at the end of my road.

Mancuso was known for playing entire records from end to end and for having a state-of-the-art sound system. From the DJ booth, he controlled the sound, lights, and even the room temperature. He wanted to create an atmosphere that would move the dancers and transport them. He played mostly R and B, the music of Motown, and the Doobie Brothers. The Philadelphia International band MFSB's "Love Is the Message" was a regular favorite, and he most famously introduced American audiences to Manu Dibango's "Soul Makossa." The 1982 rap cover by Nairobi and the Awesome Foursome, "Funky Soul Makossa" became a hip-hop, B-boy-B-girl anthem, and Dibango's song was eventually sampled by both Michael Jackson and Rihanna.

In 1970, *Soul Train* debuted in Chicago, and once it became nationally syndicated, creator Don Cornelius moved it to Los Angeles. Dance music and free dancing were coming out of the underground and into the national spotlight. *Soul Train* showcased R and B and soul music and musical performances by nearly every popular artist of the day, such as the Commodores, Earth, Wind & Fire, and the Jacksons, but what it is most known for is the dancing. It was the first show to feature Black teens doing Black dances on television for a national audience. *Soul Train* ran from 1970 until 2006. Sponsored by the Johnson Products Company, a Black-owned business, which was also out of Chicago, *Soul Train* was "the longest running, first run, nationally syndicated program in American television history" until 2018.

Dancing became one of the most important ways that young people expressed themselves, and they would follow where the music led them. Dance clubs and discos started opening up all over the country, particularly in New York. Mancuso set the standard, and other early pioneers followed, including Nicky Siano, Larry Levan, and Frankie Knuckles.

NICKY SIANO AND THE GALLERY

Nicky Siano grew up in Sheepshead Bay, Brooklyn. He started hanging out in the Village because it was a relatively safe place for young gay people. In 1969, when he was fourteen years old, he was going to Mancuso's parties.

In an interview with Jeff "Chairman" Mao for *Red Bull Music Academy*, Siano recalls what it was like for gay people in the seventies and how dance clubs were a place of safety:

> There was a lot of prejudice still going on, very prejudiced, New York in '72. It was hard for gay people. The nightlife became a place where the disenfranchised gathered and supported each other in their day-to-day lives. It was really hard for Hispanic [and] Black people. Every disenfranchised group was in the club at one point or another and the thing about the Gallery was that it didn't matter: gay, straight, Black, white, Asian, it didn't matter. You were accepted 100 percent and you were never . . . there was never a fight. There was one fight in seven years that we operated, one fight.

One of the things Siano learned from Mancuso was that a party was built on music and a sense of community more than anything else. People need to be accepted in order to feel accepted. The other important thing he learned was how to build an atmosphere that could get the crowd moving and take them to the next level. In 1973, after working as a DJ in a club called the Enchantment, Siano borrowed money from his older brother, bought a loft space, built it out, and opened a club modeled after Mancuso's Loft parties, called the Gallery. He hired a young Larry Levan and Frankie Knuckles as decorators and light men, and booked artists like Grace Jones and Loleatta Holloway to perform. He brought in a third turntable to add sound effects and create the mood in the club. He became one of the top DJs in New York. When the Gallery closed in 1977, Siano became one of the first DJs at Studio 54, and he is still active today. In 2014, he made a documentary called *Love Is the Message: A Night at the Gallery*, directed by Jim Bidgood.

LARRY LEVAN AND THE PARADISE GARAGE

Larry Levan is one of the earliest pioneers of dance music and one of the most beloved DJs of all time, a visionary artist and a guru of sound. He helped develop and design sound systems for nightclubs that have been replicated all over the world. He was a natural. He was the first "Super Star" DJ and the first to remix and extend records for the dance floor.

Born Lawrence Philpot in Brooklyn, New York, on July 20, 1954, Larry Levan was a complete creative. Well-known for his fashion and his wild, colored hair, he designed his own clothes (his mother was a dressmaker) and worked with other up-and-coming New York designers to create looks that set trends in the underground scene before the birth of punk and punk fashion. He not only played records and designed entire club's sound systems, but he also crafted lighting and decor that created a complete ambiance in the space.

Levan and Frankie Knuckles became close friends in high school, and as teenagers, they first experienced the club scene together. They attended parties at Mancuso's Loft and were part of the Ball Scene (the LGBTQI fashion shows and performances that created the dance style known as "vogueing"). As artists, they developed their skills together, learning from one another along the way.

Frankie introduced Larry to Nicky Siano, and they started working at the Gallery, doing lights and decor. Siano taught both young men the basics of how to spin records and how to use the equipment. Like most geniuses, Larry learned quickly and soon developed his own style, focusing on creating sonic narratives that took the crowd to new heights. It wasn't long before he and Frankie became resident DJs at the Gallery and developed a loyal following.

Larry replaced Siano as the resident DJ at the Continental Baths, a gay bathhouse in the lower level of the Ansonia Hotel on Manhattan's Upper West Side; Bette Midler got her start there, with Barry Manilow as her piano player. In several interviews, Frankie describes how he worked the lights and how, when Larry took extended bathroom breaks, he would have to take over the turntables.

Frankie described Larry as "a perfectionist in every way," and he talked about how Larry would go to extremes to make sure the vibe was just right. Famously, he would stop in the middle of a set to adjust the speakers or the lighting. He would even polish the disco ball, the crowd waiting patiently and cheering when he finished. Larry wasn't known to play for the crowd. He played what he liked to hear and was all the more revered for it. Some of his sets included songs like "Right in the Socket" by Shalamar, "Take Me Home" by Cher, "Paradise (Reach for the Sky)" by Change, and "Trans-Europe Express" by Kraftwerk.

When the Continental Baths declared bankruptcy and closed in 1976, Larry became the DJ at Richard Long's SoHo Club. The following year, Michael Brody and West End Records owner, Mel Cheren, opened the Paradise Garage. They created the club around Larry and built it to his specifications. Richard Long, a premier designer of dance club sound systems, worked with Larry to design and install every aspect of the lighting and sound. This was revolutionary because no club had ever been designed around a DJ and because the sound system itself was the first of its kind. Long created the Bertha speaker for Larry, then designed and named the "Levan Horn" bass speaker for him. The Paradise Garage had the best sound and biggest dance floor in all New York; it could hold up to two thousand people. These innovations transformed the dance club experience and are the model for how modern clubs set up their sound systems today.

Anything Larry played turned to gold. By the 1980s, he was a world-famous producer, remixing artists like Grace Jones, Duran Duran, Gwen Guthrie, Nami Shimada, and the Peech Boys. Record labels gave him the newest music, and as disco moved into the mainstream, radio DJs developed their programming around his set list. He used reel-to-reel tape players to edit his own tracks and to build new music in the moment. His innovations even influenced record companies to create the twelve-inch single, which extended tracks, specifically for the dance floor. (West End Records was the first label to make a twelve-inch with the vocals on one side and an instrumental version on the other).

Larry was the resident DJ at the Paradise Garage from the time it opened in 1977 until it closed in 1987. He traveled the world as a producer, DJ, and sound-installation consultant. (For example, the Ministry of Sound, UK, wanted to model their club after Paradise Garage and hired him to help them install their system.)

When he was asked in a 1990 interview with Nohashi Records about the kinds of places he likes to work in, Levan said he preferred to spin in bars or clubs, "with no alcohol, no air conditioning, because people who would endure that, are sincerely there to dance and party." He added, "That's my function, to make people party." When asked what advice he would give to young producers, he said, "Listen to yourself. Don't let people tell you what kind of music you should do, what kind of work. A true artist is one who believes in himself, second to God. Respect yourself and believe in what you do."

Larry Levan died on November 8, 1992, just after returning home from a tour in Japan. A documentary about his life and the Paradise Garage, *Larry's Garage*, which was directed by Corrado Rizza, was released in 2020.

"RACING AGAINST THE ULTIMATE WACKNESS": HIP-HOP'S CONTRIBUTION TO HOUSE MUSIC

When discussing the pioneers of dance music culture and the roots of Chicago house music, it is important to pay tribute to the holy trinity of hip-hop, whose inventions and techniques carved a path for creating music that all musical styles have inherited. DJ Kool Herc, Grandmaster Flash, and Afrika Bambaataa are just as important to Chicago house music and to all dance music, as are Emile Berliner, who invented the record, and Thomas Edison, who invented the gramophone. Without them, we would not have the ability to mix, scratch, and sample records and extend breakbeats. (That scene in *The Get Down*, with Grandmaster Flash and the magic crayon, is based on reality.)

While disco was spreading in bars and nightclubs around Manhattan and other parts of the country, in the Bronx, Frankie Knuckles's stomping ground, they were playing some of the same music, like "Soul Makossa," without the emphasis on the vocals. In disco, the lyrics told the story. In the Bronx, "the Boogie Down," as they call it, the groove, was all about the percussion and the breakbeats.

Larry Levan left Brooklyn. Frankie Knuckles, the LGBTQI kids, and other creatives left the Bronx. They all headed to Manhattan to find freedom and self-expression. But there were young people and creatives who stayed in their boroughs who also needed safety and places for self-expression. DJ Kool Herc, Grandmaster Flash, and Afrika Bambaataa helped provide the music and spaces for the youth in those communities.

In the 1970s, New York was a dangerous place, no matter where you were. If you weren't part of the elite, times were hard. The Vietnam War was ending, and many soldiers were returning home with addictions and few opportunities. Inflation was high, people were out of work, and as a result, crime was rampant as people turned to the street economy in order to feed their families. Gangs ruled the Bronx, and shady landlords set fire to their own buildings to collect the insurance money. Black and Latinx communities were flooded with drugs as the government tried to squash Black and Brown liberation movements like the Black Panthers and the Brown Berets. As a reaction to this environment, the holy trinity of hip-hop—DJ Kool Herc, Grandmaster Flash, and Afrika Bambaataa—all threw parties as a way to gather people from their communities in peace and to provide positive outlets.

On August 11, 1973, DJ Kool Herc and his sister Cindy threw a "Back to School Jam" that has come to be known as the first official hip-hop party. DJ Kool Herc was born Clive Campbell, and he immigrated to the West Bronx with his family from Kingston, Jamaica. Influenced by reggae, dancehall, funk, R and B, and soul, he and his friend Coke La Rock used the mic to give shout-outs. They also began to use witty rhymes that got the crowd hyped up. This was the beginning of the DJ and the master of ceremonies (MC) combining their skills to fuel rap music, which eventually evolved into hip-hop.

DJ Kool Herc's main innovation was to use two copies of the same record to endlessly loop the percussive sections, otherwise known as the breakbeat, so kids could dance to it. He called this new technique "juggling," or "the Merry-Go-Round." (The dance style based on these beats became known as "breaking," and dancers were called B-boys and B-girls.). DJs across genres started using this technique to create continuous loops, extend records, and create new sounds.

Grandmaster Flash, born Joseph Saddler, is a DJ and rapper who was born in Barbados and grew up in the South Bronx. He threw parties in the parks and expanded on DJ Kool Herc's Merry-Go-Round technique. In order to find the beat on one record, so they could mix it smoothly into the next record, DJs counted the grooves or counted time and lifted the tone arm to blend. Grandmaster Flash figured out that by putting his fingers directly on the record and moving it forward and backward, he could perfectly catch the beat and loop the sound. He used a crayon or marker to mark his place, so he could find the beat's exact location each time. His technique became known as the "Quick Mix Theory" or "Back Spin Technique." He also developed "Punch Phrasing" or the "Clock Theory," where he isolated short pieces of music and used a mixer to punch over the sustained beat.

The Quick Mix Theory, Punch Phrasing, and the Merry-Go-Round revolutionized the way all DJs mixed and remixed records, and they are techniques DJs who spin wax still use today.

Afrika Bambaataa was born Lance Taylor and is a DJ, producer, and rapper from the South Bronx. He is the founder of the Universal Zulu Nation, a collective of youths and former gang members from different gangs who work together to stop violence in the community. Bambaataa and the Zulu Nation developed the four elements of hip-hop: peace, love, unity, and having fun.

Bambaataa started throwing parties in 1977 and was responsible for helping hip-hop travel out of the South Bronx into Manhattan and around the world. He and his group, the Soulsonic Force, made the classic song "Planet Rock" using the TR-808 drum machine and the same Kraftwerk song frequently played at the Paradise Garage by Larry Levan.

Technology and innovation helped both hip-hop and disco/dance music evolve. Each of these styles of music come from the same sources: R and B, funk, and soul music, a sense of community, and the creativity of Black people. Without these early pioneers of hip-hop and their techniques, house music and dance culture would not be what it is today.

DISCO DIPS BACK UNDERGROUND

Dance music morphed into disco as technology and musical innovations such as synthesizers, drum machines, over-the-top sound systems, and DJs inspired thousands of new clubs around the country. In 1977, disco exploded into the mainstream in almost all aspects of American culture, from fashion and dance to film, television, and literature. *Saturday Night Fever* and the Bee Gees' soundtrack opened up disco culture to the world. People caught the beat and wanted to wear the clothes and feel the elated experience of dancing in a club with all the lights and glamour. Let's not forget, *Soul Train* and *American Bandstand* were coming into people's homes nationwide every Saturday afternoon at this time. After a hard week at work, people wanted to cut loose and do it in the open. Housewives wanted to hustle, and hustlers wanted to boogie.

When Steve Rubell and Ian Schrager opened Studio 54 in 1977, they modeled it after the Loft, the Gallery, and Paradise Garage. They combined all of the sound elements (Richard Long also installed the sound system) and the glamourous, creative decor, but they took away the community elements, instead adding a kind of exclusivity that was the opposite of what the other clubs cultivated. The community aspect and harmonious love for one's fellow humans did not exist at Studio 54; the star-studded snobbery at the door was part of the attraction. People came from everywhere to be there, sometimes waiting out in the cold for hours to see if Steve Rubell himself would pick them to come in. His goal was to diversify the club but only according to his particular taste in the moment.

One of the most famous and sampled songs from the disco era is Chic's "Le Freak," which the band wrote after they had been denied entry to Grace Jones's birthday at Studio 54, even though they'd been invited. They went home and began a groove, using the hook "fuck off." Realizing that it was a good song that could get radio play, they changed the lyrics, and the rest is history. (A number one, hit song is always the best shade, in my opinion.)

It has been said by many artists interviewed about the disco era that Studio 54 exemplified everything that was wrong with disco. While the rest of New York and other places around the country were starving, these folks were passing around the plate and feasting on cocaine. While we can't blame the decline of disco solely on Studio 54, its mainstream popularity inspired record companies to produce some terrible music that oversaturated the market. Artists soon stopped wanting to be associated with disco. Black, Latinx, and LGBTQI folks found their spaces overrun with newbies looking for that *Saturday Night Fever* vibe, so they went back underground.

Studio 54 closed in 1980 after the owners were arrested for embezzlement. Hip-hop began to move into the mainstream, and punk emerged into alternative music spaces. Some white rock fans resented Black, Latinx, and LGBTQI folks for making money and gaining fame, out in the open, everywhere. They resented these groups taking up spaces they felt once belonged to them. Record companies saw a decline in record sales and quickly dropped artists and stopped making disco records aimed at the mainstream.

Larry Levan was still drawing huge crowds at Paradise Garage up until the day it closed in 1987, due to the fatal illness of one of its owners, Michael Brody. Frankie Knuckles was beginning to make a name for himself in clubs all over town as well. Meanwhile, in Chicago, promoter and businessman Robert Williams wanted to open a new club. The DJ he had in mind was Larry Levan, but Larry did not want to leave New York and his residency at Paradise Garage, so he told Williams to ask his good friend Frankie Knuckles. The Warehouse opened in Chicago in 1976. Frankie Knuckles moved to Chicago and became the musical and creative director at the Warehouse in 1977. House music was on its way.

SHARON WHITE

Women not only wrote, produced, and performed house music, they played and promoted it as well. One of the first (if not the first) female DJs of the disco era was Sharon White. Her career started in 1972. As an African American woman spinning, producing, and promoting music in the 1970s, she paved the way for other women in the music business. A trained musician, she studied percussion at the New York School of Music from the age of seven. She wrote music and played guitar and drums in high school, focusing mostly on British rock, blues, and folk. She earned her BA in communications from the New Institute of Technology, becoming a radio engineer and on-air personality her freshman year.

Sharon played all over the world, including in New York, Washington, DC, San Francisco, London, LA, and, of course, Chicago. She held residencies at such clubs as Studio 54, the Limelight, the Roxy, Sound Factory, the Palladium, and the Pavilion on Fire Island. She was the first woman to DJ at the Saint. She was the only female DJ to play at Larry Levan's Paradise Garage and the first female reporter for *Billboard* magazine. Sharon worked as a promoter for RSO, Motown, Island, and Polygram records and worked with many artists, including Thelma Houston, Rick James, Teena Marie, Linda Clifford, Bonnie Raitt, the Commodores, and Run-DMC. She retired in 1994 but returned for the love of music ten years later. She said in an interview with "discoguy" that she now plays "a mixture of Trance, Tech-Funk and Tribal." As one of the pioneers, we owe a great debt to DJ Sharon White.

Chapter 3

THE ORIGINATORS, 1976–1989

The late sixties and early seventies were a time of social and political turmoil, economic challenge, and prolific creativity in the city of Chicago. Despite the Civil Right Act of 1964, things were still difficult for Black and Latinx people and immigrants. Mayor Richard J. Daley was smack-dab in the middle of his twenty-one-year reign (1955–1977). Backed by his close connections to Hubert Humphrey, Lyndon B. Johnson, and the Kennedy family, along with the politically influential South Side Irish community, the first Mayor Daley had enormous power. He and his political cohorts were called the "Chicago Machine" and were known nationwide for their strong-arm tactics and corruption. They controlled who got elected to local and national office, and they held tight control over who received the money and resources that flowed through Chicago. In the days following the assassination of Dr. Martin Luther King Jr. on April 4, 1968, the city erupted in protests that burned through major neighborhoods on the majority-Black South and West Sides. In forty-eight hours, there were over thirty fires, and eleven people died. Mayor Daley called in ten thousand police officers and seven thousand

National Guard troops to take control of the "arsonists and looters" and the political protestors. He ordered soldiers to "shoot to kill arsonists" and "shoot to maim or cripple looters." The Austin and Lawndale neighborhoods on the West Side, and Woodlawn on the South Side, were nearly burned to the ground. There were food shortages, and thousands were left homeless. Rather than send in funds to help the suffering rebuild those neighborhoods, Daley bulldozed them and divested public and private funds, leaving the communities looking like wastelands. Many of the bulldozed piles of rubble, vacant lots, and abandoned buildings remained for over thirty years. Some of those same areas are still blighted today.

In August of 1968, Chicago held the Democratic National Convention, where police brutalized hundreds of Vietnam War protestors. The convention helped bring major construction projects into the city like O'Hare International Airport, the Sears Tower, McCormick Place Convention Center, the University of Illinois Chicago, and the Dan Ryan Expressway. Racial politics still deeply informed decisions about the direction the city was taking. The new Dan Ryan Expressway was rerouted through the middle of two Black communities, Douglas and Grand Boulevard, in order to segregate them from the South Side Irish neighborhood, Bridgeport, home of Mayor Daley and his family.

Mayor Daley and his machine worked actively against integration. They were responsible for developing the largest concentration of public housing in the country, the Robert Taylor Homes, and for expanding Cabrini Green, the famous public housing project on the city's Near North Side. Daley used public housing to further segregate the city's growing Black and Latinx populations, and his policy of redlining sealed the deal.

Under Daley's watch, on December 4, 1969, the day before I was born 1.3 miles away, fourteen Chicago police officers and the FBI collaboration, COINTELPRO, broke into Chairman Fred Hampton's apartment. Unprovoked, police fired over one hundred shots, killing Mark Clark and wounding Brenda Harris. Using an informant, they drugged and assassinated Black Panther Party chairman and Rainbow Coalition founder, Fred Allen Hampton Sr., while he slept in his bed with his pregnant girlfriend. Chairman Fred Hampton successfully unified poor Blacks, Latinx, and white people, fed over three thousand hungry children per week, and was making strides on a national level. He was twenty-one years old when he was assassinated.

The early seventies saw the Chicago Stockyards closed down, along with the steel yards and other manufacturing plants. "The Great Inflation" and the oil crisis pushed Black, Latinx, and working-class folks further to the edge. Yet these same economic, social, cultural, and political struggles helped fuel a revolutionary onslaught of creativity in Chicago. During this era, musicians and artists were making a new kind of soul sound, inspired by James Brown and led by Curtis Mayfield. Artists like Ramsey Lewis, the Emotions, Earth, Wind & Fire, and Minnie Riperton gave young people grooves to dance to and theme music to lead their civil, revolutionary actions. Jessie Jackson formed Operation PUSH (People United to Save Humanity, now called the National Rainbow Coalition/ Operation PUSH). The Black Arts Movement fueled a new sense of pride and helped develop new creative outlets, with organizations like OBAC (Organization of Black American Culture) and AfriCOBRA (African Commune of Bad Relevant Artists) leading the way. They were creating new, African American aesthetics, and Chicago was becoming a haven for Black intellectuals. People were segregated, but they were partying in their own homes, taverns, and clubs. There was not yet a rainbow coalition or loft party scene, but Robert Williams would soon help to change all that.

ROBERT WILLIAMS

When businessman, DJ, promoter, and Warehouse creator-owner Robert Williams came from New York to Chicago to visit in the early seventies, he found the scene to be highly segregated and "tired." He was a regular at David Mancuso's Loft and the Gallery, but he found nothing like those clubs in Chicago. While there were musical innovations happening, nothing in the club world compared to the proliferation of dance clubs and the music scene happening in New York.

Williams was born in Jamaica, Queens, New York. He went to law school at Columbia University and trained with the Dance Theater of Harlem. He worked for the New York Department of Probation at the Spofford Juvenile Detention Center in the Bronx. It was at Spofford where Williams met Larry Levan and Frankie Knuckles; Williams was their counselor. One night, Williams spotted Larry and Frankie out at a club called Tamburlaine and questioned the teens about being out at two o'clock in the morning. They quickly clapped back, asking Williams if he had to work in the morning. After a little playful "blackmail," the three came to an "I-won't-tell-if-you-won't-tell agreement." Larry and Frankie then took Williams to a refurbished church that had been turned into a club called the Sanctuary, where they smoked from a hookah and listened to Santana. After that night, the three became lifelong friends.

In the mid-seventies, Williams moved to Chicago to live with an aunt. His fraternity brothers and other friends wanted to start throwing parties. Knowing Williams had knowledge of what was happening in New York, they asked for his advice. In an apartment on Belmont (on the North Side), they set up rented speakers, made crepe paper decorations and spiked punch, and threw a successful party that was quickly broken up by the police due to noise complaints. Knowing they would not be able to use a residential space for future events, Williams asked if his friends knew anyone with a loft.

They found a friend of a friend who did. It was a loft space in the West Loop, at 116 South Clinton. A female artist named Max Hats agreed to rent her loft out, but after one successful party, she wanted to raise the rent, and Williams and his crew were forced to find a new spot. While walking around Max's loft, they saw a hole in the floor and noticed there was an uninhabited space below. After talking to the owners, the group rented it—it had previously been a feather factory—for $300 a month.

They spray-painted everything black, including the windows and toilet. They bought speakers and sound equipment, rented lights and a mirror ball, and threw a few successful parties. Then the whole building burned down and they lost everything.

After some interesting persuasion—you know, Chicago-style—the owner agreed to help them locate another space, and they moved their parties to the former Jerry Butler Studios at 1400 South Michigan. The spot was directly across from the fire department and drew a more diverse crowd. Remember, this was around 1975. Their group was made up of young Black, Latinx, white, and LGBTQI people. The firemen were overwhelmingly Irish south-siders (Mayor Daley's people). At one party in early winter, it got super crowded and hot inside, so they opened the windows to let in some cold air and cool things off. The steam poured out into the air, and it looked like the building was on fire. The firemen raced over and shut things down. The following weekend, one of the members of Williams's crew mooned the firemen who were sitting outside the firehouse. The next day, they found the place filled with bullet holes. Shortly after, the firemen went to city officials and issued citations for the space, which closed it down for good. Williams and his friends had only been there a month.

Their next spot was located at 555 West Adams. The crew of fraternity brothers and their friends was an informal social club called "US." Williams was not yet officially a member of the group, but when they started having financial issues involving the misappropriation of money, Williams, who'd attended law school, suggested they incorporate the group. They soon became US Studios, and they asked Williams to serve as president. He agreed, then fired half the officers as soon as he could. The fired former US Studios members formed their own group called the Bowery, and when they left, they took all of their party people with them. Williams and the remaining US Studios members kept the equipment.

US Studios found another location for their parties. It was an art deco-designed building on 206 South Jefferson, and they rented it for $650 a month. It was a three-floor walk-up with no air-conditioning, but it had possibilities. They did some repairs and sent out invitations, but only twenty people showed up. The DJ left to join the Bowery group and everybody went with him. Not to be outdone, Williams went back to New York for reinforcements.

The first person he tried to recruit was DJ Keith Scott. When that didn't work out, he asked Larry Levan. But Larry was bringing in major crowds at Richard Long's SoHo club and working on getting his own club, the Paradise Garage, so he didn't want to leave New York. He suggested Williams ask Frankie Knuckles. Frankie was DJing around town but wasn't really satisfied with any of the clubs he was playing. Williams offered him his own club, a place to stay, and at Frankie's insistence, a round-trip plane ticket. Frankie Knuckles accepted the deal and moved to Chicago.

Next, Williams asked Richard Long to come to Chicago and help him customize and design the sound system for his new club. They built out the space, with Long's custom sound system and with Knuckles as the DJ. They sent out invitations for a free Saturday night party, attempting to compete with the Bowery. It was a flop. Only a few people came, and the ones that did were not going for the New York sound or the New York DJ. Frankie suggested they go to the Bowery to check it out.

Michael Matthews, a former US Studios member and friend of Williams, was excited to have a DJ from New York in the club and invited Frankie to spin a set at the Bowery. Frankie played his ass off. The crowd loved him. Williams and Frankie threw another free party at 206 South Jefferson, the Warehouse, and it was a success. People had never heard a sound system like that, and this time, they were more open to the new music and style Frankie was laying down. Within a few weeks, the word got out and everyone started attending Williams's club, just to hear Frankie Knuckles and that tremendous sound.

FRANKIE KNUCKLES

Frankie Knuckles was born Francis Warren Nicholls Jr. on January 18, 1955, in the South Bronx, New York. He grew up across the street from Luther Vandross, and the two would ride the train into Manhattan together on the way to school. Frankie went to the High School of Art and Design, intending to become a designer. He studied textile design at the New York Fashion Institute of Technology. He grew up listening to the music his older sister played, like jazz artists Sérgio Mendes, Sarah Vaughan, and Stan Getz. He was also highly influenced by R and B groups out of Philadelphia, like the O'Jays, the Spinners, Harold Melvin and the Blue Notes, and MFSB, and Motown artists like the Isley Brothers, the Temptations, Smokey Robinson, Marvin Gaye, and Ashford & Simpson (who eventually became his mentors in the music business).

He met Larry Levan in eleventh grade, and the two started hitting the club scene, the emerging ball scene in Harlem, and getting into trouble.

They regularly went to places like Tamburlaine, Better Days, David Mancuso's Loft, the Gallery, and the Sanctuary. They even spent two weeks in the Spofford Juvenile Detention Center in the Bronx, two blocks from Frankie's house, when they were fifteen or sixteen. After clubbing one night, they were hanging out when they saw a donut truck that was parked while making deliveries. They were hungry and decided to sneak in the back and grab some snacks. As they gleefully ran down the street, donuts in hand, they literally ran into a police car. While they were in the detention center, they met Robert Williams, who was their counselor and only a few years older than they were. It was the last time Frankie was ever arrested.

Frankie got to know Nicky Siano, owner of the Gallery, and he introduced him to Larry. Curious, Larry was the first to ask Siano if he could spin records at the club when it was closed. Siano taught them both basic DJ techniques—how to use the equipment and work the lights. Eventually, they worked at the Gallery, decorating and running the lights.

Both Frankie and Larry practiced and improved upon the techniques they learned from Siano, spending their spare time finding new and innovative ways to create ambiance for the dance floor.

Frankie got his start as a DJ by working the lights for Larry, who was the DJ at the Continental Baths. When Larry would take bathroom breaks, Frankie would change the record. His career took off from there. He eventually became DJ at the Continental Baths on Monday and Tuesday nights; Larry worked there Wednesday through Sunday. Around the same time, the pair met sound engineer and world-renowned sound system designer Richard Long at the Gallery. They began an apprenticeship with him that lasted for five years, learning everything they could about sound and sound equipment.

When the Continental Baths closed in 1976, Frankie Knuckles worked at various clubs around New York. Larry was quickly becoming a rising star. Frankie was making a living and honing his craft, but he was far from stardom. When Robert Williams approached him to be creative director, resident DJ, and part-owner of his new club in Chicago, Frankie took advantage of the opportunity. He was only twenty years old.

Word quickly spread about the new club at 206 South Jefferson. It was a three-floor walk-up in an industrial area. There was no sign outside, but they were loosely calling it US Studios. On Friday nights, it could be rented for private parties. It was members-only on Saturday nights from midnight to 8:00 a.m. They served no alcohol. It was a gay club, and the members had to be at least nineteen. They were allowed to bring a guest, and if someone wanted to become a member, they needed to have a recommendation from five other members. The membership rules weren't intended to be exclusive; it was a Black gay club, and the rules were there to keep people safe. Through word of mouth, US Studios (the Warehouse) was the place to be on Saturday nights. Williams said in several interviews that he modeled the Warehouse after the Loft. It is with the same spirit of inclusion and connection, based on love of the music and the strength of the LGBTQI community, that the Warehouse became legendary and crowned Frankie Knuckles as the godfather of house music. And as the club's popularity grew, the crowd began to get more diverse.

By 1981, people were going crazy for the kind of music that you could hear at 206 South Jefferson. In an interview with Jeff "Chairman" Mao during a Red Bull Music Academy lecture, Frankie Knuckles recalled when he first heard the term "house music." He was riding on the South Side with a friend and they were at a stoplight when he noticed a sign in the window of a tavern called the Bitter End that read "We Play House Music." Frankie asked his friend what it was and his friend replied, "That shit you play down there at the club." His friend explained that the kids' nickname for the club was the Warehouse, and since it had no sign and was in the warehouse district, the name made sense. Frankie said, "That was the first time I really felt like I belonged in Chicago. That I was part of the city. The fact that people had given it a nickname, that they thought of me and that music together, all in one." Owner Robert Williams liked the name and adopted it for the club. That is how the Warehouse got its name and how the music played there was christened house music in 1981. Like the essence of the party and the message in the music, it was named by the community it served. That's such a Chicago thing.

By 1983, Frankie and Williams were having "creative differences." Frankie got the opportunity to open his own club, and he took it. In the fall of 1983, he opened the Power Plant, a nine-thousand-square-foot space at 1015 North Halsted. He asked Williams to be a part of the new club, but Williams declined. Without a DJ, Williams closed the Warehouse, but he still had a few tricks up his sleeve. He was going to open a new club.

Williams opened the first Music Box in February 1983 in an industrial building at 1631 South Indiana Avenue. It was in a relatively secluded area, near the Yellow Taxi Cab Company. Initially, Williams was the DJ, but the crowd followed Frankie to the Power Plant. The first Music Box only lasted a year because the building was being condemned. In 1984, Williams found another location, beneath the city in a gritty area filled with loading docks and yellowed steel beams. It had been a club called R2 Underground, at 326 Lower Michigan Avenue. Williams was forced to change the name from the Music Box to the Muzic Box because a historic movie theater on the North Side, called the Music Box Theater, already owned the name. Eventually, Williams took the other company to court, citing the fact that the other venue had "Theater" in its name. He was eventually granted the right to change his club's name back to the Music Box. (Though there was never any sign, just "326" spray-painted in orange outside. Most of us locals just called it "the Box" anyway, due to its boxlike shape inside.)

Trying to find a way to compete with the Power Plant, Ron Braswell, Williams's friend and the manager of the Music Box, recommended a young DJ who was spinning innovative music with a distinctive style, and who had his own loyal, local following. His name was Ron Hardy.

While Frankie Knuckles was earning his undisputed title as the godfather of house music, Ron Hardy had been DJing in Chicago for many years and was quickly becoming house music's guru. Wherever he played, his flock followed. His wild, uninhibited style, high energy, experimentation, and openness made him one of the most sought-after and beloved DJs around Chicago, even before Frankie came to town.

RON HARDY

Ronald Randall Hardy was born in the Chatham neighborhood on the South Side of Chicago on May 8, 1957. Much about his private life remains private. He started going to clubs and moved out of his parents' house at seventeen. By nineteen, he was the DJ at the Jeffery Pub, a Black gay bar on the South Side. He moved to Los Angeles briefly and returned to Chicago in 1981, playing regularly to a steady crowd at the Ritz, located in the Rush Street/Gold Coast neighborhood. He was the Wednesday night DJ at a gay club in the Old Town neighborhood called Den One. (It was renamed Carol's Speakeasy in 1978. While it remained popular until 1991, it closed in 1992. It was never able to recover from the stigma after Jeffery Dahmer picked up one of his victims, twenty-three-year-old Jeremiah Weinberger, there in 1991.)

Ron Hardy and Frankie Knuckles met while Ron was the resident DJ at Den One, and they became close friends, sharing music and learning from one another. They were the two top Black (and gay) DJs in the city for a very long time. Den One and the Warehouse were sister clubs.

People would go to Den One first, because it closed earlier, and then go to the Warehouse after-hours. While their fans may have fiercely taken sides, Frankie and Ron were the best of friends, and they never felt like they were competing with one another. They had very different styles and played to different crowds. Frankie's crowd at the Power Plant was more "grown and sexy." People dressed up, and the crowd was a bit older, usually between nineteen and thirty-five. In fact, there was an unofficial dress code. They wanted to keep it "classy," and Frankie laid an artistic, groovy sound, blended with a lot of soul.

Ron's crowd, on the other hand, was young and wild, mostly gay, and mixed with all kinds. The Music Box was more "come as you are," and it had no need for the fancy. You were going to come out of there drenched with sweat and wrinkled anyway. Ron's style was definitely high energy, and you could hear just about any kind of music coming out of his speakers. People in Chicago will still get into heated arguments about who was the better DJ. I call them the Frankieites and the Ronettes. For the most part, though, it was just a matter of taste.

When Frankie Knuckles opened the Power Plant, he offered Ron a DJ slot. Around the same time, Robert Williams offered Ron a chance to headline at the Music Box. In a 1995 interview with Frank Broughton, Frankie talked about the advice he gave Ron Hardy. He said, "I really think you should go ahead and do it. But go in there with your eyes open and mind sharp." He said, "Don't work with a half-assed sound system. . . . Tell them this is what you want and this is how much money you want and this is what you need in order to do your job here."

As the resident DJ at the Music Box, Ron Hardy brought in an electric energy. Using two turntables, a mixer, and a reel-to-reel tape recorder, he created fast-paced, pitched-up, looped edits on the spot, earning the nickname Ron "Heart Attack" Hardy. He'd often start his twelve-hour sets with "Welcome to the Pleasuredome" by Frankie Goes to Hollywood, and from there, he would play almost anything, from anywhere—from jazz, Bessie Smith, and Ray Charles to Rudy Ray Moore, Melba Moore, ESG, Shalamar, Patti LaBelle, and Sister Sledge. He was a risk-taker who would use the sound of the needle hitting the side of the record at the end of the song in his mix. He'd use sound effects like trains and airplanes. His most famous technique was turning the needle upside down, putting the record on a thimble, and playing the underside of the record, which would play the song backward. Ron knew how to flip a beat on its head.

He was open to new artists, and if someone brought him a song he liked, he would play it on the spot. If he was breaking a song, he'd often play it three or four times during the night.

He broke some of the most iconic house music songs: Marshall Jefferson's "Move Your Body—The House Anthem," Chip E.'s "Time to Jack," and Larry Heard/Mr. Fingers's "Can You Feel It." Unfortunately, very few of Ron Hardy's own mixes were captured on vinyl, but there are some bootleg versions of his Music Box sets available on YouTube.

By the time the Warehouse closed and the Power Plant and the Music Box opened, there were juice bars, clubs that didn't serve alcohol, and other new clubs popping up everywhere. New wave (punk-out music) and Euro disco were being played on college radio and by one of Chicago's most influential radio personalities, Herb Kent (the Cool Gent).

HERB KENT

Herbert Rogers Kent was the "longest running DJ in the history of radio." He was nicknamed "the Cool Gent" and "the King of the Dusties," for the smooth R and B and soul he played through most of his career. He started in Chicago radio back in 1944, when he was sixteen years old, playing classical music on WBEZ Chicago. In the early eighties, he hosted a radio show called *Stay Up and Punk Out*. He played music from bands like Devo, the B-52s, Haysi Fantayzee, Depeche Mode, the Thompson Twins, the Police, and the Waitresses, and he had a huge influence on Chicago teens. Many DJs and producers from Chicago house and hip-hop credit Herb Kent with influencing their musical taste. One of the most versatile media personalities, Kent was the host of the very popular *Steppin' at Club 7*, a dance program on WLS-TV in Chicago in the mid-1990s. He died after his morning broadcast on October 22, 2016. The Cool Gent was certainly one of the originators who laid the groundwork for house music in Chicago.

PAT & VERA

The most legendary of all Chicago female party promoters are community activists Pat McCombs and Vera Washington. They founded Executive Sweet, otherwise known as "Pat & Vera Parties," a "traveling club" for women of color with a newsletter with over 1,500 women subscribers.

Originally started in 1979 by Pam Turrell, DJ Sheron Webb, and Pat McCombs, Executive Sweet was rebooted in 1982, with McCombs and Vera Washington at the helm. They set out to create "a place for women to come in and enjoy themselves, and be entertained at the same time, in a safe environment." It is one of the oldest and largest women's parties in the Chicago. Initially, they held parties three times a week, then held monthly parties in different venues around town, as well as on cruises, out-of-town trips, and hotel dances. Currently, they hold a few major events every year. They specialize in "providing women with a variety of venues for socializing and networking" as well as "opportunities for cultural displays of art, arts and crafts, vendors, publishers, writers, health care educators, entertainers and politicians" in conjunction with their events.

They invite the most beautiful, professional women they can find to their parties. They are spectacular, lush events, held in venues where the women feel comfortable being themselves among other Black, professional women, and where the owners are respectful of lesbian women of color. Women dress up and come out in droves.

Executive Sweet started as a response to the discrimination Black, Latinx, and other women of color felt at male gay bars, as well as at lesbian bars, which primarily catered to white women. When they tried to get into certain (white) bars and clubs, they were asked for passports and sometimes double or triple identification. Some clubs were even more degrading. They would ask Black and Latinx women for "green cards," which were cards given out to public aid recipients. Some bars and clubs simply denied them access altogether.

Pat McCombs was instrumental in helping to change these discriminatory policies in bars and clubs throughout Chicago. She began by organizing a boycott of CK's/Augie & CK's, one of the most notoriously racist lesbian bars in the city during the 1970s and 1980s. When a friend was asked for a "green card," Pat led a march against the bar. She then formed an organization called the Black Lesbian Discrimination Investigation Committee (BLDIC). They found a lawyer and took their complaints to the liquor commission. They staged sting investigations and boycotts with white allies, sending both white and Black women to bars in order to find out which ones were being discriminatory, and then reported those venues to the liquor commission. The boycotts and the BLDIC investigations led to the better treatment of all LGBTQI people of color in bars and clubs across the city.

Both Pat and Vera have been active in the community for decades. Pat was a special education teacher for thirty-six years. She was a member of the NAACP, the Southern Leadership Conference, and Yahimba. In 1986, she organized the women of color tent space at the Michigan's

Womyn's Music Festival. She is also a member of the steering committee for Chicago Black Gays and Lesbians, a board member for Windy City Black Pride, and a volunteer for Affinity Community Services, Literary Exchange, the Lesbian Community Cancer Project, and Women of All Colors and Cultures Together.

Vera Washington has been volunteering since she was fourteen years old. She currently works as a case manager for HIV-positive and post-incarcerated women, and for women in the sex trade. She is also a program manager for Prologue Alternative High School and the Safer Foundation. She volunteers for Windy City Black Pride, Affinity Community Services, Literary Exchange, the Lesbian Community Cancer Project, AIDS Foundation of Chicago, Youth Pride Center, the United Way, and the American Red Cross.

In 2000, Pat and Vera were inducted into the Chicago LGBT Hall of Fame.

DJ LORI BRANCH/DJ RAPTURE

The early house scene in Chicago spawned DJs like weeds. Promoters were hosting teenage parties all over town, at high schools, in people's homes, and at clubs like the Loft, the Penthouse, the Aragon Ballroom, and Sauer's. House was becoming a culture that had its own style of dress, and people were forming social groups and collectives that had dance teams, which naturally included a DJ or two. The Chosen Few was one of the first, but there were many others. One social group, called Vertigo, nurtured Chicago's first female house DJ, Lori Branch.

Vertigo was made up of Branch, Jean Pierre Campbell, Eric Bradshaw, Jose Gomez, Steven Moore, and the producer Craig Loftis. Beginning in 1980 and continuing through 1984, DJ Lori Branch and the Vertigo collective hosted parties and performed every week in DJ battles around the city for teen crowds. She helped pave the way for other women and became one of the most sought-after DJs, male or female, in the city.

She took a break from spinning between 1985 and 1991 to pursue her degree in arts and media management at Columbia College Chicago. In the nineties, when she returned to the turntables, she broke new ground once again, becoming one of the first female hip-hop DJs in Chicago, performing under the name DJ Rapture with the group He Who Walks Three Ways. The group featured the godfather of Chicago hip-hop, Duro Wicks, the musician, writer, performance artist, and social justice activist; Juba Kalamka (Juba Johnson); Ron Clark; Ethan McClendon; Paris Brewer; and me. (Yes, I was part of a hip-hop crew too.) DJ Lori Branch, Duro, and Juba opened for groups like A Tribe Called Quest, Arrested Development, the Fugees, and the amazing Meshell Ndegeocello. In a unique position, she held residencies, spinning both hip-hop and house at many clubs around Chicago, like Red Dog, Union, Paris Dance, Augie & CK's, Avalon, Estelle's, Berlin, Shelter, Cairo, and the Cotton Club.

In 2014, she was inducted into the Chosen Few's House Music Hall of Fame. She is a board member of the Modern Dance Research and Archiving Foundation and cohosts the *Vintage House* show on WNUR 89.3 FM Evanston/Chicago and WNUR.org.

DJ CELESTE AND THE FANTASTIC FOUR (PLUS ONE)

The Fantastic Four was the first all-female house DJ collective. It started in 1982 and included Celeste Alexander (DJ Celeste), Khrishna Henderson (the First Lady), Berlando Drake (Bird), Kenya Lenoir, and eventually a fifth member, Angela Hurley (Steve "Silk" Hurley's sister). The protégée of Andre Hatchett, one of the biggest and most humble

Chicago house DJs, Celeste and the Fantastic Four were established as the female version of the Hot Mix 5, and they were part of the exclusive DJ team for promoter David Risqué's GUCCI (Gentleman's Unification of Conceptual Individuals) Productions, which included Andre Hatchett, Steve "Silk" Hurley, and Keith Fobbs.

In 2009, DJ Celeste became co-owner of Sophisticado Recordings, and in 2011, she was named one of the top one hundred most influential DJs in Chicago house history. In 2015, she was inducted into the DJ Hall of Fame, receiving the Frankie Knuckles Achievement Award. She plays various festivals and events, including the Chosen Few Picnic, the Chicago House Music Festival, Divas of House, Herstory@ Chicago's Daley Plaza, the Annual Silver Room Sound System Block Party, and the Queens of House Picnic. She currently hosts the podcast, *The Celestial Odyssey.*

DISCO TONI

In the 1980s, a ton of people were promoting parties. The teen scene was a hot market because, at the time, juice bars were still allowed to stay open all night. Most of those venues were eighteen and over and the legal drinking age was nineteen. The rules were relatively loose, and the violence was nothing like it is today. These were safe places for young Black and Latinx kids, and most of them weren't bars at all. They were parties at rented loft spaces or high school gyms. It was the underground culture that helped fuel house music, and unlike the Warehouse, the Music Box, and the Power Plant, the people who attended these parties were mostly straight kids from the South and West Sides of the city and the inner suburbs. The main woman on the scene was "Disco Toni," Toni Shelton.

Disco Toni is a model, promoter, media personality, and talent manager from the Kenwood neighborhood on Chicago's South Side. She started throwing parties in the early eighties and has promoted thousands of events over the last thirty years. She's held her annual White Party (where everyone wears white clothes) since 2009, and in 2017, she promoted the Original Queens of House Music in the middle of downtown Chicago, at Daley Plaza.

WBMX AND THE HOT MIX 5

Shortly after house music had been christened by its godfather, Frankie Knuckles, and its guru, Ron Hardy, the Chicago radio station 102.7 WBMX-FM put together a team of DJs called the Original Hot Mix 5. Frankie was initially recruited for the group, but he found he wasn't into being a "team player" and dropped out. The members included Farley "Funkin" Keith (Farley "Jackmaster" Funk), Scott "Smokin" Silz, Mickey "Mixin" Oliver, and Kenny "Jammin'" Jason. Later, Ralphi "Rockin'" Rosario joined the crew. They played Warehouse-style mixes on the radio show *The Saturday Night Live, Ain't No Jive Dance Party*, which brought house music into the mainstream. The records they played were influenced by the music played at the Warehouse, the Power Plant, and the Music Box, but it had a more high-energy sound, with synthesizers and drum tracks rather than gospel vocals and orchestration. There was more pop to this variety of house music.

Beginning in 1983, the Roland TR-808 and TR-909 drum machines (1985) allowed nonmusicians to create beats and produce dance tracks and remixes in their houses, and it seemed like everyone in Chicago was making a song, or at least tracks for one. Because people were making music in their *house*, those in the mainstream got the idea that house music simply was music made at home. Those in the underground, and those in the LGBTQI community, knew that house music stemmed from the music played at the Warehouse because they were the ones who named it. By the mid-1980s, house music was everywhere in Chicago. Juice bars and clubs started popping up left and right. 1983 alone saw the opening of the Power Plant, the Music Box, Medusa's, and Smartbar. Some of the other clubs around town included the Candy Store, Club LaRay, and the Powerhouse. Promoters like David Risqué and Mr. Ali were throwing teenage parties at places like Sauer's, the Playground, the Hotel Intercontinental, Mendel Catholic High School, public high schools like Kenwood, Hyde Park, and Whitney M. Young, and in the disco at Markham Roller Rink. DJs formed crews and collectives and sponsored DJ battles. Chicago was house music crazy, and it was everywhere. House music migrated from the underground LGBTQI scene to the straight scene, and the popularity of house records, like Jesse Saunders and Vince Lawrence's "On and On," Chip E.'s "Time to Jack," and Marshall Jefferson's house anthem, "Move Your Body," took the Chicago house sound across the country.

THE CHOSEN FEW

Wayne Williams, a DJ and producer, created the Chosen Few Disco Corporation in 1977. By the mid-eighties, he added local DJs Alan King and the legendary brothers Tony and Andre Hatchett to create the Chosen Few. They promoted and hosted parties at Sauer's, the Tree of Life, First Impressions, the Playground, the Loft, and all the high school parties.

There were many other DJ collectives at the time, and they continue to flourish as the Chicago house scene marks it's fiftieth year.

In the late eighties, Andre and Tony Hatchett's family started having a family picnic in the gardens behind the Museum of Science and Industry. They would DJ, and each year, they would invite friends to join them. As it began drawing more and more people, Kim Parham, a good friend and the manager of the Chosen Few, suggested they make it a "reunion" of longtime friends from the early underground house scene. They started calling it the Old School Reunion Picnic. By the nineties, they'd renamed it the Chosen Few Picnic, and in early 2000, it became the Chosen Few Picnic and House Music Festival, which now draws thousands from all over the world.

CITY OF CHICAGO JUICE BAR ORDINANCES

The Music Box and the Power Plant closed in 1987. Mayor Harold Washington, Chicago's first Black mayor, enacted a city ordinance requiring juice bars to close at 2:00 a.m. Previously, if a venue didn't serve alcohol, they had no closing time and could stay open all night. The Warehouse, the Power Plant, and the Music Box were all juice bars. They also mostly catered to patrons who were Black and gay. When they were forced to close, it drastically changed the landscape of Chicago's club scene. Newer clubs like Smartbar and Medusa's played an eclectic mix of house, new wave, and other forms of dance music, and they were special in their own way, but the Warehouse, the Music Box, and the Power Plant were Black-owned and gay-owned, and that made a big difference in the clubs' flavor and vibe. The music that was created there and the community that was formed within those walls was something unique.

In 1991, Chicago proposed an ordinance that would require new juice bars to obtain special-use permits. Like waste-transfer facilities, group homes, and other institutions categorized as special use, they were required to provide parking for 10 percent of their customers, and they had to be approved by the zoning board of appeals. This ordinance effectively closed down all juice bars and underage dance clubs. Teenagers now had no place to go. (Oddly enough, 1991 was the year I turned twenty-one.)

Things really did change in Chicago after that. More teens struggled with alcohol and drug use. Teen violence increased. Without the music and safe spaces that the juice bars provided, teens had no place to go and nothing to do on weekend nights. Of course they were going to get into trouble.

THE NEW SCENE, 1985–1989

Frankie Knuckles produced Jamie Principle's "Waiting on My Angel" in 1985, and "Your Love" and "Baby Wants to Ride" in 1987. That same year, Adonis released "No Way Back," and J. M. Silk's "Jack Your Body" reached number one on the British pop charts. House music was now a worldwide phenomenon. Frankie moved back to New York and began residencies there and in London. People adored him, and no one seemed to hold it against him for leaving Chicago. He'd done a lot for the city and went on to do more great things. He recorded three albums of his own: *Beyond the Mix* (1991), which contained "The Whistle Song," his most famous track, *Welcome to the Real World* (1995), and *A New Reality* (2004). He founded Def Mix Productions with David Morales and Judy Weinstein, a collective of producers, arrangers, singers, engineers, and musicians. He remixed and produced for artists like Mariah Carey, Michael and Janet Jackson, Luther Vandross, Sounds of Blackness, Diana Ross, En Vogue, Toni Braxton, and Michael Bolton. In 1997, he won a Grammy Award for remixer of the year.

He regularly returned to Chicago for special occasions, such as his birthday party, which was always filled with standing-room-only crowds at Smartbar. On August 28, 2004, then Senator Barack Obama named the street in front of the building that once housed the Warehouse "Honorable Frankie Knuckles Way" and deemed the day Frankie Knuckles Day.

After the Music Box closed in 1987, Ron Hardy was in high demand and continued DJing at clubs and special events around Chicago until his death in 1992, at thirty-three years old. We have a special kind of love for Ron Hardy in Chicago, partly because he stayed in Chicago—and we value that loyalty—but mostly because he gave so freely to all of us. He died so young, and we'll never know what else he could have accomplished. But what he gave us has lasted decades and continues to be rediscovered by new listeners.

The house music scene changed in the nineties and early 2000s. It was no longer just a Chicago hometown thing. DJs were superstars, and new clubs were no longer bare-bones spaces with state-of-the-art sound systems. They became giant showrooms with bottle service and small dance floors. When Larry Levan, Frankie Knuckles, and Ron Hardy first started DJing, they didn't expect they could make a career out of it. Now, DJs are jet-setting all over the world.

House music's roots and influences stem from many sources, but its creation, development, early evolution, and its unmistakable sound must be attributed to the originators: Larry Levan, Robert Williams, Frankie Knuckles, Ron Hardy, and all of the early DJs and promoters. We must also give credit to the fans, who gave house music its name.

Chapter 4

THE INNOVATORS, 1990–2000

By the 1990s, hip-hop and house were seemingly in competition in Chicago. Radio stations that had once been champions of house music changed their formats to hip-hop and R and B. Early on, both the house and hip-hop communities were blended, with most of the same people going to the same parties, but the nineties saw a distinct divide as hip-hop tried to forge its way in a house town.

By that time, house music was an institution in Chicago. Everyone knew what it was, though not everyone agreed about where the name came from and what its future should be. People still don't agree about those things, or about what "deep house" is. If you ask fifty people the same question about Chicago house music, you are going to get forty-seven different answers. But that's family, right?

There are those who took old-school (ole'-skool) or early house music, studied it, and made whole new communities out of the principles of acceptance, peace, love, community, and freedom, and translated those into the hip-hop scene that was just beginning to take hold in Chicago.

Some people even defected and left house music altogether. Some straddled the fence. Either way, the nineties were definitely a time of transition.

There was an outburst of new music from around the country, and because Chicago is right in the middle, it pulled from all of those influences. The East Coast had hip-hop on lock, but in Chicago, artists like Da Brat and Twista were making names for themselves, and a young Common (Common Sense as he was called back then) had a big, loyal, local following. An equally young Kanye West was also already considered a local master beatmaker.

The West Coast had grunge, and California had hip-hop and indie pop. Chicago added to that mix with industrial music put out by Wax Trax! Records and Ministry/Revolting Cocks member Al Jourgensen. Smashing Pumpkins, Material Issue, and Urge Overkill rose from their weekly "3 Bands for 4 Bucks" shows at Cabaret Metro to national fame. Artists like Liz Phair topped the indie-alternative rock charts.

The Innovators, the fourth- and fifth-generation house community, mixed the new neo-soul with Afro-beats and created expanding sounds. These are the people who grew up with house music as an established community and art form. Though it was recognized worldwide, it was still a somewhat underground culture in Chicago. The Chosen Few turned their family picnic into a homecoming for the larger house community, and it created a kind of house music renaissance in the city of Chicago. New female DJ crews, like Superjane, were making waves, and private members-only groups, like 3 Degrees, were holding weekly parties that promoted unity and gave the die-hard someplace regular to go, unburdened by the elitism and "bottle service/VIP culture" that seemed to be overtaking the clubs, making the dance floors almost undanceable.

The club boom that started in the late eighties continued throughout the nineties and early 2000s. These new clubs were no longer holes in the wall, with sawdust on the floor for dancing. They were massive spaces, often with multiple rooms that hosted a different DJ in each one. The state-of-the-art sound systems and extravagant decor attempted to bring a new kind of sophistication to club life, which meant long lines, expensive drinks, and an obsession with VIP status. It was almost as if Chicago was trying to be like its big sister, New York. Several New York-branded clubs opened up in Chicago. The Limelight was short-lived, but Shelter and Crobar reigned for many years. The Generator and the Prop House were the premier Black, gay clubs and were almost exclusively house clubs. Zentra, the host site for 3 Degrees parties, and Red Dog had hip-hop and house music on alternating nights. The owners of Cabaret Metro and Smartbar opened a smaller, more intimate, live music venue in Wicker Park that often featured what was the most innovative event of them all, live band house music from artists like Peven Everett and New York's Tortured Soul.

As with the Pioneers and the Originators, the Innovators incorporate their love of house music with their desire to help meet the needs of the community. Here are some of those people.

3 DEGREES GLOBAL

3 Degrees Global was started in 1999 by DJ/producer Jeremiah Seraphine, Julius "the Mad Thinker," bigSexy, DJ Monna, Priti Gandhi, and early member Czboogie, as a "Wednesday night get together of friends, family, and music lovers." It was based on the six degrees of separation theory—the idea that most people are separated by six degrees—but with a twist. They believed that "like-minded people are only separated by 3 degrees" (in Chicago, that might even be more like one and a half). They wanted to provide a more intimate space, closer to the early days of house music culture. They created members-only events across the city in clubs like Zentra,

Betty's Blue Star Lounge, Slicks, Smartbar, and RednoFive. A member could bring a close friend, and to get a membership card, all you had to do was ask for one. The idea was not to be exclusionary. It was a way to expand circles of friends who were there for the music and "to promote unity with the clubbers, promoters, DJs and clubs." 3 Degrees' weekly parties were instrumental in bringing back the vibe of friendship and connection rather than competition, flash, and shadiness. The collective eventually grew to host member parties in Detroit, San Francisco, New York, Washington, DC, and Miami. They have over 3,100 members worldwide.

HOWARD "HOWIE/SLICK" BAILEY

Howard "Howie/Slick" Bailey worked security at the door of Medusa's back in the late eighties when he was only sixteen years old. One of the tallest people in the room, he had a baby face and an infectious smile that endeared him to everyone who met him.

Always present on the scene, he opened Beat Parlor in Wicker Park in the nineties. One of the only Black-owned, independent record stores on the North Side, Beat Parlor specialized in collectible and rare vinyl. It developed into one of the most well-known record stores in the city, particularly for hip-hop and some dance music. He had DJs spinning live in the store and was responsible for introducing the newest, latest tracks. Beat Parlor became almost like a community center for young musical entrepreneurs and artists, with Duro Wicks, the godfather of hip-hop (and house music officiant), as the store's main employee, offering advice and support.

Howard opened Slick's Lounge on Goose Island at 1115 North Branch Street, in 2000. The resident DJs were Lee Collins, Richard Waddington, and Sadar. As the name suggests, it had a cool, laid-back atmosphere, with light-colored fabric draped around the booths, exposed brick walls with paintings of the jazz greats, and blue-tinted lighting. Slick's had a jazz club feel with a house edge. They also served really good food, a slice above regular bar fare. It was one of the hottest clubs in Chicago right up until it closed in 2007.

In 2015, with his business partner Terrance Ross, Howard opened Dream Café & Grille on the South Side, in the African American neighborhood of Englewood. As a resident of Englewood for many years, Howard recognized the lack of healthy food options in this neighborhood, which has a lack of resources and a high crime rate. Located on Sixty-First and Halsted Street, Dream Café & Grille created a space for people to sit down, get on wi-fi, and have a healthy meal at an affordable price.

In an interview with Michael Gebert of *Fooditor*, Howard said, "You should be able to get a decent meal for $5. It might not be the most gourmet, but you should be able to get a good, fresh, hot meal for five bucks anywhere in Chicago." He's done outreach in the Englewood community that is centered around feeding kids at schools, promoting urban farming, providing food for community-based organizations, like the Resident Association of Greater Englewood (RAGE), and supporting art students at Little Black Pearl. He sees Englewood as being very similar to the Wicker Park neighborhood in the early eighties, and he believes that it too can be revitalized with more support, more local mom-and-pop businesses, and more community involvement.

CREATING A CULTURAL HUB: A CONVERSATION WITH KENDALL LLOYD

In the nineties, Wicker Park was the center of art, music, poetry, and culture in Chicago. Wicker Park was to Chicago what Greenwich Village was to New York in the 1950s and 1960s. Kendall Lloyd, owner of Another

Level/Literary Explosion, was basically "the Mayor of Wicker Park" and at the center of it all. Lit-Ex was the gathering place for everyone passing through, and it was the lifeblood for so many of us.

Another Level was the bookstore. Literary Explosion was the poetry/performance reading series, which continued at other spaces until 2000, even after the bookstore closed. (Everyone referred to the bookstore and the reading series collectively as Lit-Ex, 1993–1998.)

I had a chance to sit down with Kendall Lloyd to talk about his experiences with house music, the intersections between house and hip-hop in Chicago, and building spaces for the community.

MLH: Tell me about your first experience with house music. What was that like for you? Where was it? Who was there? All that.

KL: Sure. My very first experience. I had a cousin that went to high school and he was into all kinds of music, like heavy metal. We would just sit and listen to the radio for hours and just hang out, talk, or whatever. This house music started playing, and I was like, "Okay, what is that?" And he said, "Yo, this is just disco stuff." We get into it. And then from there, I started seeing it everywhere.

MLH: When WBMX started doing the hot mixes, how old were you?

KL: Oh man, I had to be twelve or thirteen. During those times, everybody had their little cassette tape, trying to make the tape mix and then bring it to school the next day. I just fell hard for it. I fell really, really hard. I got really into it.

I started seeing my older cousins and siblings, and they were into more disco stuff. They were more into the original songs, where we were more into the mixes of the songs. They were able to go out every night, and I could see them getting dressed, and we started trying to dress like them. That went on all the time, pretty much throughout most of high school, and I just started getting deeper and deeper into it. When I really got into it was at the Power Plant.

MLH: Was the Power Plant the first place you went, or were you going out before then?

KL: I was going out to high school parties. I went to Whitney Young. We had like a lot of house heads there. We had sock hops, and we would have pretty serious DJs come and spin for us. We had Keith Fobbs. We would have Craig Loftus. We had some pretty heavyweight DJs, well-known. For whatever reason, they would come in and play our parties. We had a lot of DJs at our school.

Frank Washington was a really good friend of mine who lived around the corner from me. He was actually a doorman at the Power Plant. I used to drive him to work. He would let me in.

I'm like seventeen years old, sneaking out of the the house. I'd park my car down by his house, and he would jump in, and we'd just go. I would walk in with him, so nobody would ever card me or anything like that. And at that point, I was just all in.

There weren't a lot of my peers able to go. I would come back with these wonderful stories, like, "Man, you saw Frankie Knuckles?" "Yep." "You saw Craig Loftus?" "He broke this record . . ."

True story. I had my SATs Saturday morning, and Jamie Principle was breaking his album *Bad Boy.* I thought we were gonna dip up here, see this show, and leave. Of course, you know nothing happens there until two, three o'clock in the morning.

MLH: Right, right.

KL: We go see the show, party afterwards, then take the bus down to Chicago State University. I gotta go take what is probably the biggest test of my life.

MLH: That's a long bus ride from the South Loop area down to Chicago State.

KL: Right yeah, yeah. My commitment to party . . .

MLH: Right! So, how'd you do on your SATs?

KL: Oh, that story. Not as great as I should have, or could have. I mean no regrets, because I made that decision, but I could have done a lot better. I thought about that afterwards. I was like falling asleep in between every section. I was just miserable, but it's a great story. In the end, I didn't regret it, but it was one of those things where, should I have done it? Would I want my child to do it? No.

MLH: But you were young. You don't know. You think you can, and you're not going to miss Jamie Principle breaking his new album.

KL: This was such an intimate gathering. And then for that record to go on and be such a big, huge hit for him. We had never really seen Jamie perform his music. It was just on tape. There was nothing as important.

Then we started going to the Music Box because the same people are kind of going back and forth. I missed a couple of the earlier clubs like the people talk about. But the Music Box, Ron Hardy, that was awesome.

And I think about it now, like how was I getting all my schoolwork done? I mean the commitment. I would be on the bus stop a lot of times, going to parties if my car wasn't running, I would still go. I mean I was committed.

The people in my neighborhood, they wouldn't even know, because none of them were going. It was just me and my neighbor down the street. We would hang out tough. Those were fun times.

MLH: So, you were full-on—they didn't call them house heads back then, but you were full-on into it. Did you have the hair?

KL: Oh, yeah. My neighbor used to cut my hair.

MLH: Oh, tell me about the hairdo.

KL: We had the baggy clothes on. We had the pump, you know the pompadour up there.

MLH: Did you have the slanted or did you have the box [haircut]?

KL: I had the box. The slanted came after. Those were my two introductory points.

MLH: When did you first come to Wicker Park?

KL: I came to Wicker Park for the very first time to hang out probably in 1991.

MLH: Okay. And what were the circumstances around that?

KL: A good friend of mine, James Ray, he was a photographer, and I used to work in my family's business. They had a clothing store on Eighty-Sixth and Cottage Grove. James was doing a photo shoot for us, for a magazine or an ad or something like that. We ended up clicking and bonding. He asked, "Where do you hang out?" I told him I go out here and there. He asked if I'd ever been to Wicker Park, and I'd never heard of it. I jumped in his car, we drove out there, and the first place we went to was the Rainbo Club. My very first bar. I fell in love with the Rainbo. I was like, man, first of all, the drinks are cheap.

MLH: Right.

KL: But the eclectic group of people you will see coming through there. I was like, man, this is off the chain! It was this hidden gem because you can see anybody, but I didn't see anybody I knew.

MLH: The Rainbo Club was beautiful inside. The bar and the booths.

KL: It still is. The owner, even to this day, is very adamant about leaving it like that. She was adamant about never changing. She didn't want to take her drink prices up too high, and she never wanted to fancy it up. She always wanted to stay that eclectic style. I mean she fought hard for that because that whole neighborhood is gentrified. That was the first place I went.

MLH: That's cool. Then when did you really start hanging out there?

KL: A buddy of mine, Bobby Sacks, and Dave Gandy. They used to hold these parties, loft parties. It was the original raves basically. They would bring a DJ in and spin, and there was this hip crowd, mixed races, pretty much any and everybody, everybody just cool and super stylish. So I started going to those. And I would just find myself in Wicker Park almost every night, between going to different bars and clubs, just hanging out at people's houses—a lot of artists, people would do things at their spaces.

And at this time, it was really still very underground. I mean, if I would tell people where I was going, and they would be like, "Naw, I'm not going over there." It wasn't the safest, but you know, as artists do, they found their way to that space. [Wicker Park] was inexpensive. You could get some big places, so there were a lot of students over there, a lot of artists, folks over there from Columbia [College Chicago], a lot of folks over there from University of Chicago. Just kind of one of those best-kept secrets. But then mixed in there you had a lot of artists, a lot of people that worked in the industry, chefs and hairdressers, designers, and super-creative people. They just kind of all found this space. It was pretty much like anything goes. That was just—man. Those are some of the best days.

I mean, I don't think that you can find spaces like that now. It's so hard to find spaces like that in America anymore, because they've all been just kind of found, stepped on, and repurposed to do something else. While I don't knock that—I always say, people who get it, get it. But those were special, magic days. It was pre-internet, so you could actually have a good time and you just had to remember it. Nobody was trying to take pictures of it and film it like that. You just got into it and went.

MLH: I moved to Wicker Park in like 1989, 1990. I was in school, and I got a little apartment. I think we were kind of protective of our space because it was a cool area, very diverse. A lot of different kinds of people. It was also definitely kind of shady over there. You know, activities going on, a lot of drug users and street people.

KL: And they ended up being your friends, right? Because you saw them enough.

MLH: Oh, yeah. I mean you learned where to go and not to go. You knew where the pimps and the workers went. They all used to hang out at the Hollywood Grill. If you were cool, they were cool, right? It was a very special place.

KL: A special place, special time. I can recall when there was this big artist that lived over there. His name was Happy [Jim Happy-Delpech, founder of the Around the Coyote Arts Festival], and he was selling major pieces of art. I'd never heard of them, but somebody invited me to a party that he was having. So that's when I really realized that there were two Wicker Parks.

MLH: Okay, talk about that.

KL: I went to his party. Beautiful mansion. This place had massive art everywhere. All of these people from Lincoln Park and the suburbs. They all flocked to this guy's house for this party. I was like, "Who is this guy?" He ended up being this huge international artist that just settled into Wicker Park for whatever reason. Through that crowd, I started meeting kind of more "well-heeled" people over there. That was like a whole other thing because you would get invited to these parties at these people's mansions, with these super well-known, connected artists that worked in the music industry or whatever. They were just quietly living over there, amongst everything else that's going on over there, you know? It's more like that today, with that area and that group, than when we were there. When you start peeling back the onion of that area and that community, I was like, wow, there is a lot going on over here. I'm not sure where he is now, but this guy was selling major art, and this is around that Basquiat kind of time, right? It was a lot going on with pop art and that kind of thing. It was a lot going on, and again, I would tell people like me, "You know, you should come over here." You could see super nice bands at places like the Empty Bottle. People just wouldn't come.

MLH: Yeah, because Artful Dodger was over there. Before Nick's became Nick's, it was Club Dreamers. I went to the punk shows over there. There was Estelle's. They had a different format, but it was there forever. How would you describe how Literary Explosion first got started? What was your vision? Tell me about that.

KL: I actually was invited to a space. I worked in the book business. I would sell books out of my car. I would go to a lot of festivals. I worked for a distributor, and basically, part of my pay was to vend books.

The distributor would say, "Hey, if you could find a place to vend books, I will cosign you some books." I would use my contacts because I had a lot of contacts on the South Side—people who would come to South Shore Cultural Center to do events, where people would come in to speak or they were coming to different venues. I'd say, "You know what, let me take some books." I paid the booth fees. At that point, booth fees were pretty cheap. You could get a nice booth for like $50 or $100. You could turn around and make like $1,000 in that particular festival. Very lucrative. We would work the Haile Selassie Festival. We would do a lot of the West Indian things.

It got to the point where he was like, "Let me know how you do what do you," because I was really pushing. I was selling more books than people he was distributing to at the stores.

I could just go to places and I would create these vibes with my books. I would always do something different. Something real cool. I would always have something else going on to attract people to our books. About this time, my buddy Bobby met a guy by the name of Greg Place. Together they decided to open up a hip-hop store called Triple X.

MLH: Oh, I forgot all about Triple X.

KL: Bob, Greg, and I—we would hang out like almost every night in Wicker Park. Greg had a cool apartment over there, and we would just get lost just talking and hanging out. They ended up hooking up a deal with the landlord. The space was scuzzy and beat up. So they said, "We'll do the handiwork, we'll do all the carpentry, do the plumbing, the electrical, just give us a year free rent." The landlord said, "Okay, cool." They worked out a deal. There was the space downstairs. There was a store there at the time when I got there. The landlord wanted them to evict the current guy. And he put that on them. [Bob and Greg] said, "Okay. We got it handled."

Bob and Greg came to me and said, "Hey, listen, we got a space, we know you hustle books, would you be interested in opening up a bookstore?"

I said, "You know what? Let me table that for a minute." I went to my distributor guy. I brought him to the space. It was jacked up at that point, but he could see the vision of it. And then Bobby and Greg said, "Don't worry, we will build it out for you. We'll get it, you know, habitable. Do you like it?" It came with free rent for the first year. I was like, "Yeah, we'll make it work." It was myself and my business partner Ann Marie. We basically built it out.

My distributors stocked it, and then basically, when I sold the books, I would give him a percentage of my sales. Then every month we would tally what I had left and then refresh. Then from there, to get some foot traffic, I went to this place called Spices.

MLH: I remember Spices.

KL: It was a cool poetry spot. I thought, to drum up some business, we could actually put some poetry down there. We had enough space. I went down to Spices and got Tina Howe. When I saw her, on the spot I said, "Tina, I got to have you at my poetry spot." She didn't even bat an eye. She said, "Let me know where. Let me know when." She built that thing up from like five people to—in our heyday, I think we would get like fifty people through there.

MLH: Right, 'cause I remember that. I remember thinking, "How the hell? Last month, she was just reading at Spices, and now she's got her own show!" And Triple X was where the shoe store eventually came and now it's a Starbucks [at the intersection of Milwaukee, North Avenue, and Damen]?

KL: Correct.

MLH: That whole corner was like our space, our cultural space.

KL: We used to bring the speakers out and bring books and stuff out, set the tables out. We would have bands come out like Dope with JC—they would be hanging out. We would have a bunch of skateboard kids, graffiti artists come out. I mean we would be doing it. Just like a happening, right? I used to watch a lot of Andy Warhol. My vision was to kind of create a space that was just a happening. If you were there, you saw it, and if you weren't there, you missed it.

And one thing I used to do—as I told you, my family had clothing stores—so we would always go on buying trips to New York. I'd go to New York like at least every six months. I'd go to Nelle's, MK, Tunnel.

And this is again before the internet. And every city had its own vibe, right, and New York had its thing. I would go to Queens and buy reggae records, come back to Chicago, and people's minds would be blown, because they just didn't have access to that type of music.

I remember playing Duro's party [Duro Wicks], and I couldn't even DJ, but I had records. He had Twilite Tone, who's Common's DJ. This is when he was first starting out. I would literally put the needle on a record and people would lose it. But these were like cutting-edge, right from Jamaica, straight to Queens. So, I say all that to say, a lot of the things that we were doing, I actually saw in New York and borrowed from that.

It was just a bunch of creative people, and a lot of students, and their minds were open. A lot of artists, and they were interested in doing a lot of things, and they brought in their own creativity to it, so it just became like this jambalaya, it was this gumbo of people bringing that thing. Tina was the perfect person, because she's extremely humble and she has a unique skill with people. People just meet her and love her.

She would just work it and build it, and I was like, "This is your baby. Whatever comes through that door is yours. I just want the people to have the awareness that we're here. I want them to, you know, to purchase something and then continue to come back. Basically, the door's yours because you're working to bring people in here. I'll help you print some flyers. I'll hand them out in the store, but I'm not in the street, like you are." I mean the bigger events, I would help work. But that day-to-day, she worked her butt off. She brought Mario [Mario Smith] in.

MLH: Can you talk more about the different kinds of events that happened at Another Level at Literary Explosion? We talked about the poetry readings—what other things were happening there? What other events happened?

KL: We would bring authors, like a lot of bookstores do, but we would try to bring authors that had cultural influence on younger people. So, for example, musically, we brought the Last Poets, which was one of the highlights. Mario Smith used to do this series called "Soulize with David Boykin," and they would do this improvisational jazz style. We worked a lot with the Guild Complex, with Marguerite Horberg. She would help us with projects. If we needed a larger space, she would let us use her space. She was a huge resource.

We were kind of off the grid. We were on the fringe, should I say, so when legitimate organizations would try to communicate with us, it wasn't a real conduit. When we wanted to do something larger, we could run it through Guild Complex, and that way, the artists could get paid, and that way we would have the insurance that we would need, because we would do pretty large-size events.

MLH: Were you guys a part of the Around the Coyote Arts Festival events?

KL: We were and we weren't. The younger me was like, "Yeah this is cool, we're anti-Coyote."

MLH: Okay, talk about that.

KL: We were still feeding off of the people that they were bringing into the community. We used to rock with these, these anarchist kids, this incubator of anarchists on Chicago Avenue, and we would hang out with them. They were super-cool kids, mostly from the suburbs but super radical.

Some of the things they were into, I had to say, "I don't think we need to be a part of that."

MLH: Black people couldn't get away with doing that stuff.

KL: Exactly, right. We'd want to kind of be safe. We would partner with them on things and they were like anti-Coyote, they were anti-Starbucks coming, I mean they were pretty much anti-what Wicker Park is today. We would have our own artists that would showcase their works. It would be like an anti-Coyote event. Down in our space, we would have people that were lesser known. It was pretty lucrative for them too. I mean a lot of people sold a lot of stuff. People would have little, small trinkets, things that they'd sell, because the Coyote would attract that money crowd.

MLH: I think when it [Around the Coyote] first started, it was a little more underground and it was a little more grassroots, and then it got to be just commercialized.

KL: One thing—to get back on the author piece, I don't want to leave that piece out—we had Kevin Powell. We had him come down with his book and speak. You know, and again, this is before the internet, so you actually had to put some feet on the ground to get your word out.

One thing that I always like to do is break new music for my audience. I would play these types of artists, where, if you were from Chicago, you probably had never heard of before. We would break a lot of things out of Europe, right down at the bookstore. We would help people try to educate themselves musically and get them off of what they always listen to.

MLH: Right, because you didn't have to go down to Literary Explosion to hear it. You could be walking past and the door would be open. You could be just walking past the door, and there would be incense wafting and some kind of good music playing all the time.

KL: It was a meeting space for the entire city, and I pride myself on that. I mean, I obviously didn't pick the location, the location picked me. But I didn't really think about how it was an intersection, in a sense, because a lot of people, I didn't realize until later, were from all over. I had a lot of friends that lived on the South Side, so we would pull in that group. We had a lot of students. They were from all over the country. We would have this mixture of people that were like, "Okay, I don't feel comfortable going over here, or I don't feel comfortable over there, but I feel comfortable going to this central spot." So through that, I saw a lot of relationships start and there are people that still work together today that met down in that space. And they didn't necessarily see eye to eye when they met.

MLH: That's very true. There were a lot of the "discussions." When you initially set up Literary Explosion, did you expect it was going to become this cultural center for Black people and artists and various other types of people? Did you have that in mind?

KL: I will say this, only because I had seen a successful business in my family, and I had some really good coaches, my uncles and cousins—I did feel like I had that in me. I felt like I knew how to build it. Now, I didn't, but in my mind, I had the type of confidence that you would probably say was overconfidence, but I felt like it could be done. Would I take that risk today? Probably not. I mean we had no money. We had no real structure. But we knew what we wanted to do. And I had seen it done before. So I was like, "I can do this." You know, I didn't think about tomorrow. I just thought about today. Each week we would get a little bit better. Remember, the first year, we didn't have to pay rent, so we didn't even worry about making a lot of money. I just wanted to keep my book distributor paid so he would keep giving me books. I was more interested in meeting the cool people that would come through, watching the transformation. It was the best job I've ever had to this day, the only job you could drink Guinness beer whenever you felt like it. And you could close up whenever you felt like it.

MLH: Yeah, because I remember it seemed like it was always open. If I walked past and Lit-Ex was closed, it had to be like six o'clock in the morning, and it was just closing. Honestly, I remember you being very dedicated and very passionate and always hipping me to something new, a book and some new music, some new idea, and being very passionate about it.

KL: I had a lady I worked with who brought in a whole other element. Her name is Eileen—she's from Denver. Eileen was part of the hemp movement, which sounds pretty commonplace now, but when she brought it down at that time, it was very controversial. It was kinda on that legal line, and, of course, you know this isn't the West Coast, this is the Midwest. She would have clothing made out of hemp. She would have a lot of books that discussed the hemp movement. They were basically trying to take people from cotton to hemp. She was, like, way ahead of her time with this stuff.

So she came down. We worked out a negotiation, and I let her bring her products down, and that was super educational for me. I know it was a weird look for people, because she was a little older Caucasian lady and here's me. I can just imagine what was swirling around people's heads at that time.

MLH: I think people were open. It was bohemian right, so she was kind of a hippie old white lady and people probably thought, on one hand, "What is this hippie old white lady doing here?" and on the other hand, they were like, "You kind of belong because we're all weirdos, so what the hell."

KL: Right, so you've got this dichotomy of stuff, because one hand, you got this Black Power Movement, then here's this white hippie lady with this hemp. And again, at this time, this is the Midwest. These were kind of new ideas. It's not like you see it now. I got some heat from some of the old heads that would pull me to the side like, "Bra, what are you doing, you can't find a sister to come down and do that stuff?" And I will be like, "You give me somebody that's plugged into the hemp community like she is. She's bringing something to the table that is unique to me—I haven't seen it." And eventually, I saw them kind of start to get it. Some of the stuff that she was turning me on to just mentally, I was just like, "Wow, okay, you on a whole other platform with it." She was really teaching me stuff.

Eventually, her and Tina became roommates. It was just a lot of that kind of stuff, where relationships were being formed, and people were getting turned on to a lot of new and different things. That was really what I wanted out of it. That was my mission. I mean, I just liked to kind of push the button, to sit back and just see what happens. That was a high for me. I mean everything else was gravy, but that was the meat to me. You have these people like, "I hate white people, white people, white devils" or whatever, and then they do poetry together, and then next thing you know, they will come down, and they will be doing duets.

MLH: Right, and couple up, living together, got a baby.

KL: And I will be like, "Wow, you know, I had something to do with that." That was such a good feeling. That was such a wonderful feeling to me. That I was doing my favorite part.

MLH: What year did Another Level at Literary Explosion open?

KL: What year? Technically, '93.

MLH: When did it close?

KL: We left there in '98.

MLH: Wow. Why?

KL: So, there was a landlord issue, where he would not renew my lease, and I was having a lot of issues and problems with plumbing. Plumbing in that whole neighborhood was crap. So if you were below sea level, it was really bad. At this point, Triple X left. It was just me. We're holding it down. Business was doing very well. He just would not renew our lease.

MLH: Because gentrification was starting to happen then.

KL: For sure. What I didn't know was that the same landlord, who had talked to them about partnering up and then building out that space and the one from downstairs, had partnered up with Flash Taco. He built that out, and he gave him the downstairs space, our space, because he wanted to do the Underdog [a hot dog place]. I was watching it, but I didn't really know what was happening.

So by the time I realized he was not going to renew my lease and that I was just gonna be month-to-month until I wasn't, I tried to move out of there. Yeah, that was a bad time.

The rents in Wicker Park were so incredibly high. I just didn't want to take a risk. We went to the South Side, tried that for a little while.

I always kept track of where people lived, and this was an interesting sociology lesson. So probably, of the people that live in the city, 60 percent of them [his customers] live on the South Side. So we do have a South Side following? And if we open up a space on the South Side, we could get more space, the rents are going to be more in line with what we want to spend.

That was not the move, because I realized that people that were from the South Side we're leaving it for a reason. They didn't want to really hang out on the South Side.

So it just wasn't right. I gave it some thought, but I should have done a little bit more research just to see, put out some feelers. Like, "Hey, if I open up a shop on the South Side, would you come support it?"

MLH: Where was it, the shop that you opened on the South Side?

KL: Seventy-Fifth, and I can't recall the cross street like, Seventy-Fifth right off of King Drive.

MLH: Okay. Yeah, so there's a whole crowd that was hanging out in Wicker Park that was not coming over there. I mean, some of us would roll because we rolled down there anyway.

KL: It didn't have enough connectedness. I look at Hyde Park—if you've been in Hyde Park, it has a connectedness. So you go over there, and Eric's got his spot over in Wicker Park and it had connectedness.

MLH: Silver Room was in Wicker Park for a long time.

KL: I was so happy. Eric [Williams], that's my guy. One of the smartest businesspeople that I've ever met.

MLH: I think the Silver Room took over where Lit-Ex left off.

KL: Exactly right. And I'm so happy. I felt like the vanguard was in good hands because I knew Eric Williams was going to take it to the next level.

THE INTERSECTIONS OF HIP-HOP AND HOUSE: A CONVERSATION WITH EDGAR "ARTEK" SINIO

On the forefront of the intersection between Chicago house and Chicago hip-hop, Edgar "Artek" Sinio is an icon in both scenes, in Chicago and internationally. He started "606 Tuesdays" at the famous Wicker Park club Subterranean in 1996 and ran it until 2006. He cofounded the hip-hop group the Pacifics and was their main producer, sound engineer, and stage DJ, under the name Projekt: PM, with releases on Guidance Recordings and Crucial Sounds.

His house and dance music DJ name is B: PM. He lives in LA and is a producer and musician who has been working with the Black Eyed Peas for many years.

MLH: What are you doing now?

ES: A bunch, but I'm still in the entertainment field. I'm not really DJing, unless it's a special thing. I didn't really want to focus on that after leaving Chicago and moving out to the West Coast. I kinda had to start over again. I left Chicago to continue making music, so I decided to not focus on being a DJ anymore and put everything into making music and production.

I ended up with the Black Eyed Peas, which is crazy, you know—I almost kind of made it happen. I remember back in the days when we first got hold of the group and realized one of the members was Filipino—turns out he's Black and Filipino. So I remember back in the days, listening to their stuff, and me being part of a hip-hop group that had the same goals. It was like a little inspiration.

I remember saying, back in the day, "Oh, that's cool. One of these days, we're going to work with them."

MLH: Wow, you just said that off the cuff and manifested it?

ES: Yeah.

MLH: That's amazing. But I could see you doing that because of all that you were doing, even back in the day, at Subterranean and with the Pacifics, who were my faves. The Children of Reality were my second faves, and then He Who Walks Three Ways. So I could see this for you.

I feel like you were really part of the intersection between hip-hop and house music. How do you feel about that? How was that experience for you, and where do you feel like you fit in it?

ES: It was very interesting, because I did kind of led two lives back then. I even had two different names to separate myself. When I was doing house music, of course, I was B: PM or Projekt: PM, and then for the hip-hop stuff, I just used my graffiti name, Artek, and that's how it's stuck. I'd do two different parties, but I didn't want to confuse the people. Because at that time, there was still kind of a separation of house and hip-hop.

MLH: Definitely. Other people have talked about that. Going from being a B-boy into being house and this sort of change in style that includes personality too.

ES: Yeah, I mean that was the thing I also remember about it. Early house parties, there were always B-boys there. House music was playing, and there were always B-boys in a circle, breakdancing, doing their thing. So to me, it was always intermingled. It wasn't until I left the city that I realized that it just wasn't like that. It was only like that in Chicago.

MLH: Okay, so that was a unique Chicago thing?

ES: Yeah, yeah, definitely.

MLH: Okay. I'm going to get to the question about how it's different in a minute, but I want to ask you about your first experiences with house music. When was it? Where was it? Who was with you?

ES: I'd say the early, early stuff. I would have to say this is before I was a DJ. So this is pre-1986.

MLH: You were still in high school?

ES: Yeah, yeah, it's pretty much like that transition between junior high and high school. And I have to say, Joe [Vergara] is probably the guy that introduced me to house music and the radio station, because WBMX to me, that was the holy grail. That's the one that you would go home and put in your cassette and record it, and you just listened to that all day. So to me, that was my early, early experiences of house music, and just to music in general. It kind of led me to pretty much everything I do now. To me, that was the beginning. Before that, especially listening to the radio, when the DJs are spinning, it's not like they're saying, "Oh, this is this song and this song." It's just like, well, this is just a good-ass song. I don't know what it's called. So it wasn't until I started DJing and collecting records that I was just like, "Okay, these are the titles," and it made me look for the titles instead of just being a listener.

MLH: How did you make that transition into DJing?

ES: To me it was easy. I don't know what it was. I mean, the early days would have to be my cousins Joe and Audie Vergara's neighbor, Noel.

MLH: Oh, "Cousin Noel"?

ES: Yeah. He was a DJ at the time, so that was our early exposure to it. I'd just seen it on TV before that. To me, the first thing that made me want to DJ was Herbie Hancock's "Rockit." It was DXT, the DJ that was scratching, that made me go, "Wow! What is he doing?" Before that, my parents didn't let us touch the records.

MLH: Yeah, you're supposed to handle them a certain way.

ES: It was funny because growing up, we were always surrounded by people that went to parties, and I remember me and Audie, every time we'd go to a party, we'd always end up hanging out with the DJ for some strange reason. To me it was like, forget the party. I don't even care about these people at this party, but this DJ is doing some cool things. They've got some cool equipment. They get to play with records. So it became a thing between me and Audie.

Actually, Audie started first. He was neighbors with Noel, and he would just go over there all the time and ask, "Hey, Noel, can I play with your equipment?" So Noel would teach him. Not too long after that, I would hang out there too. I picked it up pretty quick.

And then years went by, that's probably in '86, when I started fooling around with turntables. But even before that, it's kind of funny, one of my toys growing up was a turntable. And then a karaoke machine. So it's kind of funny what I do today.

MLH: Right. Your parents knew you were gonna be going in this direction at a young age.

ES: Yeah. So, it went from there. I started hanging out, and then I think it was about '89 when I really started seriously getting into it. I had friends that already had equipment, and they started DJing in their basement. I would frequently go over to their place just so I could practice. And then in '89, I decided to hit up Noel and asked him if he still had all the equipment. Because at that time, he wasn't DJing anymore. It was just collecting dust in the basement.

MLH: So you got equipment from Noel, then where were the first clubs that you went to, and where were the first places you DJed?

ES: I remember doing mixes and the soundtrack to what the cheerleaders were working on and what the Poms [the Bolingbrook High School Pom-Pom Squad] were doing.

MLH: That's actually very cool. You must have been very popular.

ES: Yeah, I mean, people were definitely jealous and had envy because the whole team would come over for real.

MLH: And the Pom-Pom Girls were cuter than the cheerleaders too.

ES: Yeah, yeah, they were. It actually worked out for me, because half the team I'd been going to school with since forever, so everybody knew each other. I was doing that, and they would have little after-sets for the basketball games, and they would actually pay me.

MLH: Oh really?

ES: Yeah. And then they would pay me enough where I would go rent the equipment like the speakers and then still make money for myself.

MLH: Wow. They were paying you really well. You are so enterprising. At that age, we were messing around. You were about your business.

ES: (Laughs) From there the raves started, and then we were going to those. It turns out I was neighbors with the guy throwing them. I mean, Bolingbrook out of all places, you know? The first person that threw a rave is from Bolingbrook. He went by Mr. Happy at the time.

MLH: Ah, okay. That's funny.

ES: I'm trying to think of what the actual company was.

MLH: Raves, that's kind of a different scene, right?

ES: Yeah, it was a different scene. We first got into it, right before the rave scene, it was the Underground's [parties] pretty much. To me it kind of morphed into it, because it was pretty much all the same people that were doing the Underground. It just kind of elevated into it. But I remember also, back then—to get back on that topic of hip-hop and house meeting—back then, when the underground house parties were happening, the underground hip-hop parties were also happening in Chicago. A lot of the people that would go to the Underground also went to the hip-hop functions. So, to me, that was kind of intermingling already.

The same B-boys that would go to the hip-hop shows would go to the house shows and would be B-boying at these house functions, so it was intermingling at that time. Then it just kind of morphed from underground into the rave scene, where I guess it was still very underground.

The money situation really changed the whole underground scene. People were like, "Nope, we're all raving now." People were making a lot of money. I just can't believe how much money. The craziest part to me was, a lot of the people running the scene weren't even twenty-one.

MLH: People needed a place to go, especially after Medusa's closed. I think that pushed the rave scene even further because when there was Medusa's, they even had the younger, under-eighteen and over-eighteen times, and kids had a place to go. They could dance. They could have good music. They could socialize. When Medusa's closed, where were they going to go? A lot of the underage juice bars closed, so then you could get into young people's pockets. Young people would still want to go out.

ES: Yeah, definitely. I say with Medusa's being closed, that was a pinnacle change from the club life back to the streets, to the underground. Because I don't really remember anything after Medusa's for a while.

MLH: There was nothing. I mean, there were still the loft parties going on, then I think the rave scene kind of took over that.

I really do see you as an innovator. You've had a lot of irons in the fire. How do you see yourself as part of the house community? Where do you see yourself situated in that?

ES: I helped kind of add color to the house scene. I mean, it was pretty colorful in Chicago, I'll admit that. Yes, predominantly Black, but of course, you know, it's created on the South Side. But from what I've witnessed, it really became a colorful, very colorful community.

It's kind of funny, in today's times, with all the gay-lesbian liberating things happening that we didn't have back then, the house scene was a free, free world, and you didn't really have to worry about that when you're in that house culture. To me, that community was something that I would like to be part of. I felt the love coming from everybody, no matter what. That was the thing that I love the most.

I liked DJing in that world because it didn't matter who you were, just as long as you felt the vibe. That was amazing. That was purest to me—before festivals, before corporate came in and started saying, "Hey, we can make a lot of money off of this."

MLH: Talk about that. Talk about how festivals have changed house music functions.

ES: I'm happy that it can generate that much money now. But at the same time, the rave scene that I witnessed will never happen again. It's a completely opposite world from where it began. It began with kids breaking into warehouses, throwing a bunch of equipment in there, and rocking it out all night. Now we need permits, we need sponsors, we need employees, it's all this craziness that it's become more of a business. It's not about that pure vibe of everyone just getting together and just dancing. It's different. It's still kind of there, but definitely it is clouded.

MLH: Now it's the celebrity DJ.

ES: It's definitely interesting how that culture elevated the DJ to crazy heights. I'll admit a lot of these celebrity DJs make so much money it's ridiculous. And a lot of times they're not even doing anything.

MLH: They get to travel the world and it's not like they're carrying crates of records. I carried crates of records for people. I'm happy that DJs are finally getting their due, because I think in the past, they didn't really get paid a lot and they were the people bringing in the crowd. Some of them deserve it.

ES: Yeah, I say some, some of them deserve it. There are some definite names that deserve it, but you know with me being in the industry, meeting some of these people, I could say it gets very "Hollywood," even though it's not like Hollywood. It's not all what it really seems to be, and there's a lot of people pulling strings for these celebrity DJs. There is a lot of behind-the-scenes that people don't realize. There's sometimes someone behind the curtain doing something.

MLH: Kind of like the *Wizard of Oz* thing?

ES: I've learned about celebrities these days, I'm just like, "Wow, okay."

MLH: I'm tempted to ask you about a DJ that I really like, but I don't want my bubble to be busted. I was obsessed with King Brit forever. "The Sound Architect," he's for real, right?

ES: Yeah, he is for real. Yeah, yeah, he's produced for so many people and done production for himself. He's up there.

MLH: Okay, good.

ES: He's one of my inspirations too.

MLH: Your experience of house music and hip-hop in LA—how is that different from Chicago?

ES: In LA, it's definitely different. In Chicago, it's more like they have taken the nineties golden era of hip-hop and they've used that as the base. So, to me, in Chicago, it is still very hip-hop. Even though there's still the youngins that are doing the new stuff. I don't know if it's because it's just a working-class environment.

MLH: Is it different in a good way? Or is it that people in Chicago are stuck?

ES: I mean, I say it's both. Because I can look at it as, well, people haven't progressed, but at the same time, I think about the sound of hip-hop in Chicago. There is a particular type of vibe that happens, and I think it's just due to the fact that we are surrounded by New York, the South, and the West. We've always got everything kind of fed in, where you go to New York, it's a New York bubble. They only listen to New York. LA, same thing. I could talk to people in LA about old hip-hop from the nineties from New York and they're like, "What is that?" I'm like, "What? Are you kidding me?" But now I realize they were definitely in a bubble on the West Coast. Which is understandable. They definitely had a lot of artists coming out here. That's what they were paying attention to.

MLH: So then with house music, how is it different in LA?

ES: Actually, house music here in LA is actually thriving. It became one of the places where, if you want to listen to some house, you could probably find it on a good night. There's a lot of DJs that come through here. Even a lot of DJs we still remember come out here on tour. So yeah, it's kind of thriving, and right now, there's a resurgence of house music, which is kind of cool because for a while, when we would go out, I was tired of hearing that big room festival stuff. I'm tired of it. It's like everybody wants to hear the same thing. So, it's kind of cool to be able to hear good house. It just kind of sucks that quarantine [COVID] kind of killed it. Right before quarantine, there were these little house functions that were starting to happen. So yeah, house music was definitely making a comeback. Even on Spotify.

MLH: Is there a scene in LA at all?

ES: Yeah, there is a scene. It's not like the underground scene [in Chicago] at all. I would say it's far from that. A lot of things are in the usual functions and venues, or little hip functions, almost typical for LA's kind of standards. So it doesn't have that same grit. That's the only way I can explain it.

MLH: So they're not having any of that in LA? It's more glittery?

ES: Yeah, it's very shiny here. "Oh, it's nice. It's so nice. Damn, they have lovely artwork on the walls."

MLH: Internationally, what has been your experience of house music?

ES: It's been nothing but love to be honest. I remember when I was still DJing frequently, and I was traveling a lot, house music brought me to all these places. That's what they wanted to hear. It's kind of cool that I got to witness and kind of bring Chicago to all these different places.

MLH: Did being from Chicago give you clout?

ES: Oh yeah, definitely, especially in the house world. Pretty much for anyone that was working at the time, that was traveling or DJing heavily in the clubs, it was pretty much respected everywhere. It was amazing how much love we would get.

MLH: Where are some of the places? What countries? What cities?

ES: Barcelona. The Philippines.

MLH: Where in the Philippines?

ES: Actually, they took me all over. It was kind of funny because I had some contacts at the time, and I just put it out there. I said, "I DJ all the raves in the US, and I'm coming out to the Philippines and would like to try and possibly do something out there." And just on a whim, I took one crate of records. I'm like, if anything happens, I'm going to have my crate of records, and pretty much—two weeks—I met people from MTV, other promoters. Then the promoters that I reached out to, well, first, they tested me out.

MLH: How did they test you out?

ES: They wanted to make sure. It was actually me and Audie, we were in Makati, and it's a little bar area. It was kind of indoor-outdoor. A bunch of bars and you could hang out outside. People are drinking outside, whatever. But me and Audie hear house music in the distance. And we say, "That's dope, that sounds familiar. Let's go find that bar." So we went to that bar, and that's where I talked to this DJ who actually turns out to be part of one of the biggest promoters in the Philippines at the time.

I basically told them, "I'm Projekt: BPM from Chicago," blah blah, did the whole spiel. And he goes, "Ah, I think I saw that in a magazine." I'm like, "You probably did." And he said, "Oh, well, me and my guys do a radio station." I think it was on Wednesday nights or something like that. He's like, "Come by Wednesday, spin a couple records on air." So they're testing me. They're like, "Do it live, yeah. Do it live, on the radio." I wasn't even thinking about it at the time. They told me later on about it, that they were testing me.

MLH: Were you geeked about it, or were you terrified?

ES: Oh no, I was like, I'm cool! On the radio! In the Philippines! All right, I'll do it! I remember going and they're just like, "Yeah, just put on two records, just put out two records." By the first record, I'm already doing things they've never seen before. And at that time, you know, Chicago was known to mess around with the e-cues and make it sound like it's phasing. While I was doing that, the phones lit up. All these people call in like, "What is he doing? What is he doing?" They had no idea. They're like, "We don't know what he's doing." So, I kind of helped bring that Chicago DJ style to the Philippines at that time.

MLH: Wow.

ES: And all their DJs were there, and they're just like, "What is he doing?" After the second song, they're just like, "If you want to keep going, go ahead." I finished off the rest of the night.

MLH: So epic.

ES: Yeah, I finished up the rest of night, and then afterwards, I had to explain to them what the hell I was doing and show them all what I was doing. And then they're like, "You know what, next week we're supposed to fly out to a different island. We're going to knock off our guy. You're taking his ticket." The following week, I was already flying to different islands to DJ at the clubs. It turned into, "We got a party next week, or this weekend. We're going to take you there." So the whole month, they just brought me around the islands and I DJed everywhere. They took me to other radio stations to get interviewed. I was like, "Man, this is great."

MLH: That's amazing. You just instantly made yourself a huge career in the Philippines just from your skills. I can't believe you were like, "I'm just gonna take my records on a plane to the Philippines and see what happens," and then end up on the radio. That's amazing.

So what other places did you DJ internationally? Where were other places you experienced house music?

ES: Spain was amazing to me, especially Barcelona. And it sucked at that time because I was going to Columbia College [Chicago], and they have a really strict policy for attendance. After five days, they're allowed to kick you out. Especially with their semesters being so short, I'd already hit my limit. So I went to Spain, and I'm like, all right, I can go to Spain, but I got to come right back home. So basically, I spent more time on the plane than in Spain. I remember pretty much the next morning, when they were taking me back to the hotel after the party, the promoters said, "Hey, you want to stay for a couple of days?" I said, "Oh, I can't. They're gonna kick me out of school."

MLH: You're so good! You actually went home?

ES: I went home.

MLH: You're so good! I would have just been like, "I'm staying in Spain. I'll figure it out when I get back."

ES: I probably should have. I had such a great time, though, the little time I was there. That was one of those special times. It's kind of like music was the language. Because when I got off the stage, I didn't understand anybody. I was like, "Nobody speaks English?"

It was interesting to see music just being the language. Afterwards, everyone was just thanking me and congratulating me. I was like, "I don't know what you're saying right now." And you know, the Spanish was different than the way it's spoken here, you know? It's not Mexican Spanish. So I kind of understand, but I don't.

MLH: You already had some fame and stardom as a DJ, not as a hip-hop DJ but as a house music DJ. You could have been like superstar, superstar, superstar big if you wanted.

ES: Yeah, I thought about it, but definitely when the rave scene started turning more corporate, that to me was the beginning of the end. That's when I started transitioning out of it. And then also, at the time, I was already starting to DJ different places in Chicago. I was kind of like, "I already got gigs, I don't really need to go after that." I just kind of got tired of it. It was just too much, and then it was very competitive, you know, because people are making a lot of money.

MLH: Was it cutthroat?

ES: Oh, yeah, especially amongst promoters. Oh, it was terrible. They're all like cool with each other, but the moment they turn around. . . . I've seen promoters take other promoters' flyers and just toss them in the trash. I don't know how many times I've seen that. And I'm just like, "Wow, you guys are supposed to be friends."

MLH: Yeah, not when it comes to that cold hard cash though, right?

ES: Yeah.

MLH: Thank you, Edgar! This has been really great. Sorry, nobody calls you Edgar anymore.

ES: Actually, all the people that really know me still call me Edgar. Yeah, historical times back then.

MLH: Yeah, you're legend. We're like the second generation of the core foundation of what has now become this global phenomenon. I don't know if you really look at it like that. I mean, you're a pretty humble dude.

ES: I've definitely thought about it. I talk about it all the time, especially now having a daughter, I always talk about how our generation was creating it, and the generations after that just kind of refined it, but we're the ones that created it. She is a product of our generation.

MLH: Is your daughter, Elle, into it?

ES: Yeah, she's into it. And she's trying to play guitar and everything too.

MLH: Oh wow. That'll be interesting to see what happens with this next generation.

ES: Yeah, oh yeah, definitely, we'll see. I'm happy with the young generation right now, with music. Music is kind of coming back.

MLH: What do you mean?

ES: I'd say that young generation of eighteen- to twenty-two- to twenty-four-year-olds—those artists are making quality music again. They are writing good lyrics. Lyrics are coming back. There's so many young up-and-coming artists that are really making waves. It's cool, and it's getting more colorful.

MLH: What's next for you?

ES: I have a couple of projects that I'm working on with Apple. And we've got a semi-instrumental album. There's still going to be some artists on there, but not every song is going to have an artist on it. I wanted to be able to use that stuff and possibly get placements. It's a streaming world, right?

MLH: That it is. Thank you so much. It's been great talking to you, Edgar.

SUPERJANE

Following in the footsteps of early eighties originators like the Fantastic 4, Superjane is the second all-female DJ collective to come out of the Chicago house music community. Founded in 1997, it is made up of Colette, DJ Heather, Dayhota, and DJ Lady D. These ladies wanted to "prove that women DJs were not just a novelty act," and they have become worldwide superstars in the process.

Colette and Dayhota met in 1995 through the loft party scene. Heather and Dayhota were roommates, and Lady D came aboard a little later. With

Heather as their mentor, Colette and Dayhota began practicing together, and after two years of honing their craft, they threw the first party with an all-female lineup at the Funky Buddha Lounge. After that, they hosted monthly events there, as well as at Smartbar and Rednofive. Since then, they have held residencies as a group and as individuals at all of Chicago's hottest clubs. They have toured the world together, produced and remixed for other artists, and made their own records. They have been featured in *Spin*, *Time Out*, *URB*, *BPM*, *XLR8R*, and many other magazines and news sources. Together, Superjane is a sonic boom that opens the universe for women in the music industry, particularly in dance music. As multitalented musicians and businesswomen, they have inspired and mentored countless other young women (and men) and helped spawn a whole new generation of female DJs, blowing the doors of the old boys' club off its hinges.

DJ COLETTE

DJ Colette grew up on Chicago's North Side, right down the street from the offices of the famous Gramaphone Records. At nine, she began training as a classical vocalist, and as a teenager, she began promoting parties, getting her start in house music by singing on tracks for DJ Sneak, Ralphi "Rockin'" Rosario, Gemini, and DJ Lego. She bought her first turntables from DJ Sneak and began practicing, learning from other local DJs like Heather, Derrick Carter, and Mark Farina.

She began singing over tracks she played, both solo and with Superjane, and has recorded six full-length albums—*Hypnotized* (2005), *Push* (2007), *When the Music's Loud* (2013), *Retrospective* (2017), *Candy Talk Dubs, Vol. 1* (2015), and *The Pete Moss Remixes* (2020)—the *Call on Me* EP (2010), and over twenty-six singles. In 2003, she created a song with Paul Van Dyk and Felix da Housecat that was used in Motorola's cell phone ads and won

Dancestar's award for "Best Song Used in a Commercial." "What Will She Do for Love," from her first album, *Hypnotized*, hit number one on the *Billboard* dance charts. The title track, "Feelin' Hypnotized," is on the soundtrack to the movie *The Devil Wears Prada*. This album also has her spectacular cover of Cherrelle's 1984 "Didn't Mean to Turn You On," a Kaskade mix (Cherrelle's version was produced by Jimmy Jam and Terry Lewis and was also covered by Robert Palmer in 1986). *Hypnotized* was iTunes's most downloaded house dance album in 2005.

Colette is the owner of Candy Talk records. She held a nine-year residency at Smartbar and has held residencies at clubs all over the country. She has also played Coachella and toured internationally with Superjane and another Chicago superstar, DJ Kaskade.

DJ DAYHOTA

DJ Dayhota (Shannon Ialongo) is known to spin barefoot, so she can feel the beat through the bottom of her feet. She started in the house music scene through Wicker Park-Bucktown loft parties in 1995. She was influenced by her roommate, DJ Heather, and along with Colette, she was a founding member of Superjane. She has held residencies in Chicago at Smartbar, Mad Bar, Transit, Karma, Crobar, and RednoFive. Outside of Chicago, she's played in New York, Detroit, Las Vegas, San Francisco, South Beach, Paris, Barcelona, Germany, Melbourne, and Sydney.

DJ HEATHER

DJ Heather (Heather Robinson) is one of the most-loved DJs in Chicago. Her kind, mild-mannered demeanor and genre-bending skills make her

DJ sets a unique, amazing experience. She is known as one of the hardest-working DJs in the business. She was named one of Chicago's "Top Forty-Five Artists" by *New City*, along with Kanye West and Green Velvet.

DJ Heather was born in Brooklyn, but she was raised in Chicago. She got her start playing records in a Wicker Park-Bucktown neighborhood bar called Artful Dodger. It was a pretty low-key artist hangout with cheap beer and a cool vibe. Over the years, she became known around town as a hip-hop DJ, with a regular Wednesday night set at Red Dog. Her three-year residency there helped her gain a big local following. She worked at Gramaphone as a hip-hop buyer and at local record labels, learning various aspects of the business. Over time, she began to spin mixed-genre sets, and by the time she formed Superjane, she was already one of the most sought-after DJs in the city.

She made a name for herself on the national and international scene as the opening DJ for Mark Farina's "San Francisco Sessions World Tour," and she was named Dancestar's Best Breakthrough DJ in 2002. Her albums include *Tangerine* (2000), *Dancefloor Principals* (2003), *Fabric 21* (2005), *House of OM* (with Colette, 2006), *OM Summer Sessions 2* (2007), and *Soundz* (with Johnny Fiasco, 2015).

"RAINBOW AFTER RAINBOW": A CONVERSATION WITH DJ LADY D

The fourth member of the all-female DJ collective Superjane, DJ Lady D, Miss Darlene Jackson, has been dubbed "Chicago's House Music Queen" by *Chicago* magazine. She was listed by EDM.com as one of the "top 10 black artists from Chicago." She got her start in 1995, and her first gig was spinning at the famous shoe store Sole Junkies (located in the Wicker Park space formally occupied by the hip-hop store, TripleX).

She founded and managed the DJ collective For Soul Only with Mel Hammond, Javon Jackson, and Mark Grant. A woman of many talents, she has managed her own music events and marketing group, D'lectable Music, since 2004.

DJ Lady D grew up in Washington Heights on the South Side of Chicago and graduated from Whitney M. Young High School (Michelle Obama is also an alum). She initially studied to be a podiatrist, then switched gears to follow her passions of music, writing, producing, and all things creative. She earned a master's degree in communications from Northwestern University, and while being a full-time mom, she has been a host and producer for WBEZ, Chicago Public Radio, and a contract writer and social media strategist. She's been an A&R representative for Chicago's Strictly Hype Records and a freelance writer for the *Chicago Tribune*. She's toured all over the US, Europe, Asia, Canada, Mexico, and Russia. She's played and held residencies at the House of Blues, Beauty Bar, Evil Olive, Red Dog, Berlin, Primary, Smartbar, Funky Buddha Lounge, Darkroom, Double Door, and many other clubs throughout the US. In 2018, she became the creative industry liaison at Columbia College Chicago, where she works with students at the career center to help them plan career strategies and connect them with industry professionals. She also designs diversity and inclusion programs, focusing on BIPOC and LGBTQI students.

Her music includes a spoken word album, *Poetry & Rhythm Featuring Lady D*, and other singles and remixes, including *RC Groove Featuring Lady D, Champagne Lady, Ron Carroll Featuring Lady D, Lady D Presents Mr. Egg Germ, Lady D Presents OGC, Featuring Kelly Love, Naked Kaleidoscope* (CD), *High Again* (12" EP), and *Pump Dance Part 2* (12" EP). Some of the festivals she's played include Lollapalooza, North Coast Fest, West Loop Arts Fest, WestFest, Chicago Summerdance, and Summer Solstice at the Museum of Contemporary Art.

MLH: Tell me about your first experience with house music. Where were you? When was it? And what did it make you feel?

Lady D: My earliest memory of house music goes back to 1982. I would say preemptively around '81, we were listening to Herb Kent's *Punk Out* show. A lot of those songs were sort of that precursor sound to house music, new wave. Telex, the B-52's, and Devo. New wave led right into the house music: "Time to Jack," "Jack Your Body," all of that, right. I went to Whitney Young High School, and everybody there was full-on house, like we were all already house kids. And so for me, I remember back in my elementary school, like in eighth grade, somebody used to bring a boom box, and they would have recorded the Herb Kent show, and we used to get out on the playground and we used to have a little dance party on our lunch break. We were already in that vibe, that new wave, new music, edgy, whatever it was like, we were definitely into it.

I grew up listening to a lot of everything: disco, funk, soul, rock and roll, blues, country and western. My brothers were DJs, so they had Technics turntables, Sony and Pioneer equipment. I started collecting my own music, early forty-fives.

When I was in high school, I started collecting twelve-inches and albums, and so I started building my record collection. A lot of my friends were DJs already. Freshman, sophomore year, people had equipment. There were little posses that were hanging out after school. They would get together and make mixes.

People were teaching me things on the side. I wasn't a part of the posse, so to speak, but I would come and hang out, and I would want to play, and being a girl, they would always say, "Oh, you can't play," so I never really pursued it in high school.

But we used to have sock hops at Whitney Young. The sock hops used to happen after school, like from four to six. The Hot Mix 5 would come through. Farley would come through. Frankie Knuckles would come through. We had all these people come in, playing parties in our gymnasium, and we would dance our butts off! Then, on the weekends, we would go to Mendel, we would go to the Soul Queen. GUCCI Productions would put on things. We would go to the Playground.

My friends, Fran and Kim, they were a little bit older than us, and they had cars. They could get their parents' car. And so we would all pile in and go someplace. I would tell my parents, "I'm spending the night at so-and-so's house" or whatever. That's how I got to experience whatever was happening.

Then hip-hop came along. I liked hip-hop music, but I didn't like the atmosphere of the events. I didn't like certain aspects of it. I didn't like the disrespect for women. So it could never really pull me in because I just didn't like that part. I'm a woman. I respect myself. I don't think of myself in any of the language that they seemed to be very comfortable with. I found that house music was always a salvation for me as a woman, to get the respect that I wanted, to have the community and the family that I wanted to be around, so that's why I really stuck with house music.

MLH: There are a lot of intersections between house music and hip-hop in Chicago.

Lady D: Yeah. They intersect in the sense that a lot of early house music jams are hip-hop, dance jams. When you talk about Houdini . . . and even the tempo of hip-hop at that time was a house tempo. That's why you get MC Lyte's "Lyte as a Rock," or you get Queen Latifah's "Come into My House," or even Jungle Brothers' "Girl I'll House You." That's how close they were. They were really like cousins. And, you know, the mother is disco. And they had just different fathers, I believe.

MLH : Yeah, that's okay. She gets around. We ain't mad at her, right?

Lady D: Oh, I love that. It's all about freedom, sexual freedom, and acceptance, you know, so that's disco.

So, that's the beginning. I feel like they were right there with each other. There was breakdancing, and that was all around the same tempo, and you have beats and they were just taking the drums and looping them. They had a lot in common at that time, but then they diverged on different paths. I was still checking out hip-hop and enjoying certain people, certain artists—they really were telling stories, storytellers and real rappers and MCs. So that's the difference for me. But at some point, where I really felt comfortable, fit in, felt safe, that was in house music.

MLH: So I'm going to backtrack a little bit. Did your brothers let you mess with their equipment at all, or were they were they like, "No! Get out of here"?

Lady D: Both. Initially they were like, "get out of here." But I would just observe them so much. Whenever they weren't there, I would just do all the things to make it work, and they had gotten so slick with it that they used to pull out the cords and put things in different places. And so they thought I wasn't going to be able to fix it. I would fix that right up and get it back to where it was. So eventually, they just had to acknowledge that, "Wow, you know what you're doing!" I mean, I was really young when I first started messing around with their stuff, and I probably did break a few needles or whatever, initially, just not knowing. But I was basically like, "Well, just show me, and then these things won't happen."

I was probably like three or four when I just remember opening albums, looking at the triple-fold artwork, liner notes. I was so into it; I could sit by myself for hours and be completely entertained. I was an early reader so I was reading these things. My parents could leave me alone in the basement. I would be fine with just going through my brothers' records, putting them on, listening to them, just comprehending, analyzing just what was happening and enjoying it. Seeing how things affected me emotionally differently, different music; I had a real, real visceral relationship. Music, from an early age, I could feel it. It was very tangible to me, and then having the instruments to be able to move a record around, listen to it again, pull it back, all those things. Hear the scratch, it does that, which is something that makes you a really good musician, a really good DJ, because you understand that from an early age, you can move the crowd.

MLH: I've been in the crowd and been moved by you, so I know. In other interviews, you talk about creating magical moments when you're playing. Can you talk about that a little bit more?

Lady D: What I was referring to was thinking about how you have a pool of things that you can work with. One is the music. Two is the technique. Three is the way you can put something together to make a whole new thing. And then four is presentation, just general presentation, like from one song to the next song, the blend is something entirely different. So you have all these elements that you can work with and create this sort of like "Wooo" moment. And it's exciting for me to have that happen spontaneously.

If I'm improvising with music that I don't normally put together, that becomes exciting. It is very special for me when I can do that. It takes a while to realize how that's happening and why it's happening and how you're the instrument of it. But it's the music inherently. When you pick a song to play, inherently it is because that music is already wonderful and perfect and it's already doing something for you. And so you can think about a DJ who can just play one song and present it so well and make everybody feel what that producer expressly meant for people to feel. That's one thing, and then the next thing is, if you can create an effect of adding something else to that yourself, your love for it; and then, maybe another person's beautiful perfect expression. It can be so many things, it's like rainbows. You can create rainbow after rainbow. Especially if there are lyrics. Sometimes there's a song, there are words. It's beautiful music, on its own, you can do it with music, but then also, if there's some sort of message that can just hit you at that moment, that's so right. You never know what that's going to be, what you need on that day, but sometimes, just giving people what they need is amazing. It's an amazing thing to be able to do.

MLH: Yeah, I mean, because you have a degree in health communications/ community health, right?

Lady D: Yeah. So that's what I have my master's in. My undergraduate degrees are in biology and pre-med.

MLH: And so I feel like you've taken that and have been able to turn it into something else, some other ways of building community. And you're working with students at Columbia College. You've got a record label, you've been in movies, you're doing public speaking. It's like you've found a way to bring all of these things together. How did that come about? And how do you keep the fire? You know what I mean? How do you keep it going?

Lady D: I'm the type of person that needs variety. I thrive on it, and if I can find ways, just different ways to create things, every day is a little bit different for me. I don't necessarily wake up at the same time every day. I'm not a very scheduled person. I do make the appointments and things like that, but every day is different. So if I feel like taking a course on diversity one day, I'll do that, and if I feel like reviewing my résumé and applying for something, I'll do that. There are so many different interests that I have, so every day is kind of unique, and I need that. But at the same time, I try to be productive enough to get certain things done that need getting done. I'm deadline-driven, so if I have a deadline, I'm going to hit it. If I don't have a deadline, it is going to be open-ended. So that's one of the things that I've learned to do for myself.

In terms of the health communication thing, it did all come full circle. Being able to take my gift for writing, my love for media and communication, my understanding of health and science, and topical things related to health and wellness. Actually, when I realized that I had put it all together, what I came up with is that music is medicine.

I had gone to podiatry school for two years. After I graduated from college, I was going to be a podiatrist, a foot and ankle surgeon. When I was in it, I realized that I didn't want to do it after the second year of school started. I did finish that second year, and I just thought, "This isn't for me," and so when I made that decision, it was really rough because I didn't know what I was going to do. I just knew that wasn't right. I was not thriving, I was feeling depressed, I was not opening my curtains, I was sleeping all day and it was really because it was not the right choice for me. I'm glad I didn't really succumb to that or end up in a place where I didn't want to be. Just realizing what that was, having that break away from school, opened my eyes, and so I was able to kind of turn it all around like, "Oh, this is why I didn't get up in the morning, because I didn't want to be doing that." I wanted to be doing something else more creative, more expressive for me, more in tune with my ideologies and my philosophies in life, and away from weirdly competitive people, who are competing about what? We're all supposed to be helping people.

And so it was that type of eye-opening experience that made me just adjust. When the music became present and full in my life, I began to center that experience. Boy, the joy that it gave me! The uplifting! And then when I saw what it did for other people. That was me coming into the ministry, but also, that was doctoring to other people, so I'm still doing it in a way that maybe people don't acknowledge, in that way, but I certainly see the health benefits of it. Dancing. Movement. You know, mental wellness. Relief. Release. All of those things, they're so important, and to be able to be somebody "on the pulpit" doing that. Sure, I'll take that. I love that.

MLH: One of the questions I was going to ask you is how has house music and the house community healed you? But you just said it. The universe put you in a place where you could heal so many people around the world. You wouldn't have been able to heal that many feet, in that way, but you can in another way.

Lady D: Exactly, and it would have been painful. Yeah, it's very painful to have (foot) surgery.

MLH: You were in another crew, and you are part of Superjane. How is it different working with the crew versus working solo? What that's like?

Lady D: They both worked in different ways, in the sense that For Soul Only, I would say, that we were like a consortium of DJs. Everybody had their individual career, but what we decided to do was to really support each other. So if you had an event, then we were all coming to your event. It was a matter of strength and numbers.

Javon Jackson and Mel [Hammond] and those guys—they were already DJs before I started, and when I came, we all lived together in a loft. We were in the West Loop, nothing else around really, a couple restaurants. It was like a ghost town over there, and so you could have big parties. You could have many raves. There was a juice bar called Alcatraz that was right there. So we all lived together and we were just living the DJ life. We would get up and immediately start playing music. Start DJ decks—there was like six pairs of decks there and a small production studio. And we would wake up, everybody would just start DJing. It was that type of thing, and then the day will go by and it was time to go out, and we would all go to the club. We'd go down the street to Shelter or go to the [New] Warehouse, just depending on what we wanted to do. We were right there on Randolph. It was nothing over there then.

MLH: Yeah, it was still meatpacking plants going on.

Lady D: Exactly, yeah. So it was a very fun time in our lives. We didn't really have any cares in the world. What it really came down to was, I had started to DJ, and then they were kind of impressed that I was able to command certain fees. I just was the type of person, I asked for what I needed. That was my leverage because it was such a novel thing to have a girl DJ. I mean, there was Psycho-Bitch, there was Teri Bristol, but straight girl DJs at the time were kind of few. And I was doing underground house. So I think I just used that to my advantage. I was just asking for what I want. I want $400.

I was working at the United Center at the time. I was making a lot of money working in the luxury suites, and so I didn't have to say yes to everything. I had that type of leverage. The guys were just taking anything because they wanted to play, and they had a lot more competition. I didn't really see myself as being competitive with them or anyone else, because you either want me or you don't. And if you do want me, then this is what it costs. Then the guys were like, "Wow, how do you do that? Why don't you negotiate for me?"

For Soul Only was my idea. My name, my whole thing. I said, "I'm gonna call it For Soul Only." Javon and Mel said, "Well, we all want to be down." So they all kind of nestled under me. I was like, okay, we'll talk about our events, and then I'm going to take all of our flyers and put them into a package, and then we can just hand them out at the club at the end of the night, so everybody would know where all the people are going to be. I had these marketing ideas from the get, and when people would want to book them, they would say, "You have to talk to Darlene." Everybody started getting paid better and getting much more recognition in the streets.

And that's how I ran it, and we did that for a couple years. And then I had a baby. I DJed up until maybe two weeks before I gave birth, and people still wanted me to play. I took some time off—about eight months after my child was born. I started doing part-time work for Underground Construction, which is Strictly Hype Records. They did hard house, and they needed somebody who could do promotional writing. So I just started doing writing for them. That was writing one sheets, artists' bios, and things like that. I think one of the first things I had to do was like write Ralphi Rosario's bio. First, I went from retail promotions, and then I became a label manager and then A&R, so it was really great. It was a great introduction to the business of the music, and I learned so much during those years. That's what enabled me to be able to start my own label.

That was a great education. I was able to create contacts all over the world. I went to conferences in the south of France. I was doing business with a lot of businesses in the UK. I just learned so much.

MLH: Wow. So how is house music different in other cities and internationally than in Chicago?

Lady D: It is different in a lot of ways. I remember the first time I played in San Francisco. I felt like, "Wow, they like a slightly different sound." It's house, but it's not Chicago house. Sometimes when you are in those environments, you don't know if you need to play more like them or if they will appreciate what you do. I was always a little bit hesitant to be full-on Chicago, but at some point, I learned that I just had to do what I do.

The sounds are different from region to region. I think even with my own vinyl collection, I used to separate music by region. So I would have all my Chicago stuff together and then I'd be like, "this is my East Coast stuff, this my West Coast. This is my Canadian. This is my Detroit stuff over here." And I would see the similarities. I could see that UK sounded different. I would say, even though you might put it all under the same umbrella term "house," regionally, there's changes in the sounds. West Coast—I felt like that tropical house sound was very big out there for a minute.

MLH: I don't think that ever really took off here, you know.

Lady D: No, I think we have our different tastes. But the shared common experiences of dancing together, the community that we create, the love that we see in the music, and the songs and the camaraderie—that's all the same. We come in peace. We want the freedom of expression and freedom in general, so I think that part is the same. We do not discriminate. We welcome each other, wherever we are and whoever we are. Not to say that anything goes. I think we definitely have a moral code and certain standards that we don't shy away from, and values in the way we protect each other.

It's nice that the community aspect stayed wherever it went. How Chicago house went everywhere but that core basic love stayed—that's nice. I like that. And I think people do appreciate the Chicago sound, being that it is the birthplace and where it all started.

That core community, that idea, enabled me to travel. It enabled me to tour all over the world—really, they want to experience a bit of the source. You get a bit of the source when you invite somebody from Chicago to come and play your event.

MLH: Was there a favorite place you've played outside of Chicago?

Lady D: Chicago is my favorite place. I ain't gonna lie. Oh, I love playing in Chicago. Chicago always gives me the thrills and chills.

Los Angeles was like a second home for a while. Seattle was like a second home, and then places really close by—Milwaukee and Detroit, St. Louis. Those three places. I have brothers and sisters in those cities, which is just a deep connection, strong roots, right here in the Midwest. So I love that.

MLH: In another interview, you also talked about how young people and the South Side are reclaiming it, how there's a new generation of underground youth that are reclaiming it. Can you talk about what you've seen and what's happening with that now?

Lady D: Sure. I'm trying to think exactly of the reference, but I think that at one point, we talked about the divergence, how some of the house audience went to hip-hop. That's where it was popping. The clubs were popping off. That's where the energy seemed to be trying to get up to clubs on the North Side. It was possibly problematic for folks. Some of those clubs have racist door policies. They weren't really feeling some of these just regular old people that love house music coming into the club because they wanted to keep it to themselves, or they felt like it was more special than that, or whatever. I don't know. But there were definitely clubs that had door policies that were—that I would see as anti-Black. No sneakers. No jeans—this, that, the other. Multiple forms of ID. And these weren't gangbangers, you know what I mean? It was like they didn't even know how to really differentiate or discriminate between what they thought they were keeping out and just people with jobs who just love house music and happen to be Black. I mean, we talking about college graduates [who had to] stand in line for two hours trying to get into Shelter and then just saying, "Forget it, I'll just go to this club on the South Side, and I'll just enjoy this hip-hop music." You know, at some point, people just stop trying, and they stopped caring about trying to get into these places.

And then radio didn't help because house music stopped getting play. You know, it never really got mainstream—except the house music shows, the mix shows, those kind of fell off and they became hip-hop shows. Radio seemed anti-, and people probably thought house was dead. Then you start getting the Chosen Few shows and the Chosen Few picnics coming back. It would be that one day of the year when people would be like, "Oh my god, house music! Whoo!" And so it became a like a reunion of sorts, and it just continued to grow and grow. People who said they were there in the beginning, who weren't even there in the beginning, but that's cool. It's all good. It doesn't matter. Just get in on it. They started to rediscover that it still existed.

In the beginning, they were really demanding the old house, but at some point, they started to open up to newer house music. And that's good because between the South Side and the North Side, the South Side [people] felt pigeonholed. Like they could only play a certain type of music or the people aren't gonna like it. And you know, Chicago people can be very touchy about their house music, and so yes, you will have people who will be like, "I just want to hear classics, I don't want to hear anything else." And then, I think after a while, they realized that there's so much more to it, and it didn't die in 1986, and that they could actually do more things with it. There's much more to discover, and so once they started seeing a thriving multicultural population enjoying house music, they felt comfortable. They could get with it. Then the south-siders started coming to the North Side, to the North Side parties, and it became much more integrated, which was good because, you know, we grew up on the South Side.

You know, house music was kind of a middle-class, Black family thing. Yes, it is gay. Yes, it is queer, but it's also Black kids from the middle class that sustained the house music explosion in the beginning. So it's kind of nice to see people come back into it and come back around.

And then for the Chosen Few to really leverage that popularity to boost Terry Hunter and keep his career popping—musically, all the things that he's continued to do and the growth of his career. That's enormous because Terry is one of those South Side icons for house music. So when you see something like that happening and how he's been embraced across the world, that's a good thing.

That's a really good thing because at one point, it seemed like if you were Black, you had to be a special kind of Black person to get your proper [respect] outside of Chicago. You'd have to go to London, like Derrick Carter. Spencer Kinsey did that. DJ Sneak. Gene Farris went to Toronto. So if you go, if you leave Chicago, you get bigger. If you stay in Chicago, it is apparently harder to get bigger, because we have such a hard time sometimes appreciating what's from here. It's nice when you see people from here stay here and get big here.

And so that is one of the things that I feel like just staying, you know, and showing what you can do, being from Chicago is a good thing. So I think that encourages the young people because we're not going someplace else, we're staying right here. We're leaving a legacy and we have a big footprint right here in Chicago. So when we do these events at

Millennium Park, at the Chosen Few Picnic, and young people can see these things, they see here, right here in our hometown, that there's this music. And yeah, maybe it is my auntie's music, it might be my uncle's music, but guess what, we go to this thing one day out of the year and we have a great time.

I saw that they started integrating more housey sounds into their own lexicon of what music is. Artists like Kaytranada, who does a very stylized-like version of house music that fits into [young people's] current trend or whatever they're into at the moment. It's a younger person doing house music, and his popularity is very encouraging for what house music can do and where it can go.

You have mainstream artists that have always done house mixes [of their songs] or a remix. But now you have people like Lady Gaga, who is deeply ensconced in house music in the types of music that she puts out. Ariana Grande, and now you have artists like Dua Lipa and Jesse Ware—some of these more mainstream artists doing house music, dance music. In our day, a more mainstream person may have been Kylie Minogue or Madonna.

So yeah, house music will never die because, one, it's still underground. It's never really had its comeuppance on the radio to become a mainstream thing. So it's always going to be a little cooler than everything else that's going on.

MLH: It's so lovely to see this all come full circle. Can you talk about what you're doing with the students at Columbia College and how you're bringing that all around?

Lady D: Yeah, I'm actually employed as an advisor, so I give a lot of career advice. I also design programming that is inclusive and that is based on what I see as chances to be equitable to all the student body, to encourage them to use the career services that are available to them, and to help them build pathways into their industries by creating relationships, building relationships, getting to know key players. I use my relationships with people in the industry to curate events, to bring them into the purview of the students so they can gain knowledge and insight and learn how to navigate this crazy world in terms of music, or employment, or internships, or whatever they need—to learn how to do marketing and brand themselves, all of those things.

I personally have taken on some students as mentees, so I'm mentoring and coaching people who really just come to me and say, "You know, I would like for you to mentor me." So, I don't have a formal mentorship program, but there are definitely students who have, I think, what it takes to make it in the industry, and they are already doing things, but they want some additional input and want somebody to mentor them, explain things to them. It sort of falls outside of the scope of what I would do in terms of career advising, because that's a very specific set of rules that we play by, as advisors, for the school. But as somebody who wants mentoring, that's different. I can tell you way more things as a mentor.

I also work with the Grammy program, Grammy U, the Chicago chapter. It's college level, sort of an introduction into the National Academy of Recording Arts and Sciences (NARAS) Grammys. The students get to meet people in the organization. They get a lot of opportunities to network and understand how the industry works, and internship opportunities, and a lot of professional development.

So those are just a couple of ways that I'm taking my twenty-five years of experience in the music industry as a DJ, as a producer, as a remixer, as a label owner, as a music publisher, and sharing that with people. Paying it forward. Letting them know how you get from point A to point B.

I also started, way back in the day, teaching young girls how to DJ, with Girls Rock Chicago, which is an organization that I love. I did establish the DJ training program within Girls Rock Chicago, and the curriculum that they use to train the young people. Really it's just about building confidence, about building self-esteem, and they do that through musicality. It used to always be about creating a rock band and writing a song and then performing. Then I did a workshop about DJing, and every year, they asked me to come back, and I decided we should just make it a formal program. If students want to learn how to DJ, as opposed to be in a rock band, they could specify that on their application. And so we would always have enough people to fill that part. The DJ would open the show, and other rock bands would come and play, and they saw that there's the center. You don't necessarily have to want to write that music, maybe you want to play that music.

MLH: That's amazing. I wish there had been something like that when I was that age. I'm glad that I'm getting to highlight and show the rest of the world, because people in Chicago, specifically, we make things, we share things, and we make community. And to see all of what you're doing—you are really healing us, and thank you so much.

Lady D: Thank you so much, I appreciate you. I have a collection of signed books, so I'll just leave space for yours.

MLH: Thank you.

Chapter 5

GUARDIANS OF THE FLAME, 2000–PRESENT

On February 17, 2003, club life in Chicago changed forever. E2, an upstairs dance venue above the Epitome Restaurant, had a horrible disaster that resulted in the death of twenty-one people; fifty more were injured. It was located at 2347 South Michigan, which had been home to several other clubs, like the Candy Store, Heros, La Mirage, and the Clique. According to news reports, a security guard sprayed pepper spray in the closed room as a way to break up a fight between multiple people. Still fearful in the wake of the September 11 attacks in New York, some people thought they were under chemical attack, and others became sick from the pepper spray. Some of the exit lights were too dim for people to see the exits clearly, and a few of the doors were chained shut, so people immediately rushed to the only way out, which was down the stairs and through the front door. People tripped on the stairs and were crushed under the piles of people trying to escape down the narrow staircase, out into the frigid cold.

The owners, Dwain Kyles and Calvin Hollins, were convicted for failing to keep the space up to code and were sentenced to two years in jail. Every club in Chicago came under intense scrutiny after that. Some officials used the disaster as an excuse to crack down on clubs that served Black and Latinx patrons. Room capacity was strictly enforced. Exit signs and overhead lights were so bright, it changed the spaces' ambiance. For a while, some of us just lost the urge to go out. No one should ever die at a party. The whole community deeply felt the loss of those twenty-one sisters and brothers.

Chicagoans are resilient, though, and as the nineties and early 2000s brought major economic ups and downs, the house music community continued to thrive. Party people, promoters, and DJs found new, innovative ways to carry on our traditions and invent new ones. *5 Magazine* became our major source of house and dance music news. Promoters, like Rick Martinez with Allay Soul Events and Sean Alvarez with We Love Soul, kept us in the know about local parties and events. Now, Facebook, Instagram, and other social media platforms help spread the word, but good old word of mouth is still one of the most grassroots ways to get people to the party. Tastemakers like Johney Williams, Joe Vergara, and Stacey Griffin, from my own crew, who haven't lived in Chicago for at least fifteen years, always roll into town and know what is happening and where. Once a Chicagoan, always a Chicagoan.

Chicago's Department of Cultural Affairs and Special Events hosts a monthly, lunchtime house party in the middle of downtown, at Daley Plaza in the summer. It also hosts the House Music Festival in Millennium Park, and several other house events through its SummerDance series.

During the summer, you can find house events in neighborhoods across the city. The three most famous are the Chosen Few Picnic, which takes place over the Fourth of July weekend; WestFest, which takes place the second weekend in July, and the Silver Room Sound System Block Party.

In 2022, for the first time ever, there was a charge. It is important to note that for the last seventeen years, the Silver Room Sound System Block Party had over forty thousand people in attendance, and in 2018, it was a free, donation-only event, paid for by creator and Silver Room owner, Eric Williams, with no corporate sponsorship. His vision was to create a space where Black people and other people of color in the community could have a place to gather and celebrate.

ERIC WILLIAMS

The first thing you'll notice about Eric Williams is he's a very nice person. The creative director and founder of the Silver Room, a boutique, music shop, visual art gallery, and community arts center, Eric has always been hands-on. His vision of having a positive impact on people and the neighborhood have helped the house community continue to thrive. Eric curates events and cultivates community by interacting with the people who come into his store and by going out to engage with people in the community.

When I was the director of the Chicago Community Condom Project for the Chicago Department of Public Health, I asked Eric if the Silver Room would be willing to be a condom distribution center and if he would allow me to keep a rather large box filled with condoms in the store so customers could take as many as they wanted. Without hesitation, he said, "Sure." He also invited me to distribute condoms at the annual Silver Room Sound System Block Party.

The Silver Room first opened in Wicker Park in 1997. One of the first Black-owned retail spaces in the area, it still serves as a gathering place for purchasing locally made and Black-owned accessories, books, and handcrafted jewelry. It is also a cultural space for readings, art shows, classes, and house music gatherings, and it draws people from all over the city. It moved to the Hyde Park neighborhood on Chicago's South Side in 2015.

Eric talked about the development of the Silver Room in an interview with *Do 312* ("On the Rise Chicago, Featuring Eric Williams"), noting, "I liked the idea of selling things all while connecting with people. I wanted to create a space where all my passions of art, music, fashion and community could coexist."

With a degree in finance from the University of Illinois Chicago, and a 2017–2018 Loeb Fellowship from the Harvard University Graduate School of Design, he continually develops innovative ways to bridge economic development with community empowerment.

The creator of the *Randomly Selected* podcast, hosted by Mario Smith, Eric helps promote local voices and helps keep the Black community informed. He cohosts the CONNECT Hyde Park Arts Festival, a three-day event in collaboration with the University of Chicago that turns empty lots into pop-up art exhibits, with music, speakers, and food.

Williams's biggest and longest-running event is the Silver Room Sound System Block Party. The annual Block Party hosts over 130 artists, seventy-five vendors, satellite art galleries, music, food, and activities for kids. As a direct response to try to make the Chicago festival scene more inclusive, Eric describes the Silver Room Sound System Block Party as "just a day to be yourself and celebrate the community."

In 2018, Eric Williams started the Silver Room Foundation. Its mission is "to create intentional art-centered experiences, spaces, events, and programming to increase the health, wellness, equity, and economic prosperity outcomes for communities of color on the South and West Sides of Chicago." Proximity, the Silver Room Foundation's urban planning and social-impact arm, seeks to design programs for public and nonprofit partnerships that increase commercial activity, localized investment, and economic opportunities for South and West Side neighborhoods.

His most recent venture is the Bronzeville Winery, located at 4420 South Cottage Grove Avenue, which opened in July 2022. Bronzeville Winery includes outdoor patio seating for seventy guests, music, and a full wine list.

For over twenty-five years, Eric has been bringing people together, helping bring infrastructure and economic development to underserved communities, providing opportunities to local business owners and artists, and helping the house music community continue to grow. He's hosted the Silver Room Block Party with money out of his own pocket for over seventeen years because of a love for his people. He represents the true spirit of Chicago house culture and community, and we are all so grateful.

THE MUSIC SPEAKS: A CONVERSATION WITH CZBOOGIE (CZARINA MIRANI)

Czarina Mirani, Czboogie, is the founder, publisher, and editor-in-chief of *5 Magazine*, the only publication in North America that focuses on house music, specifically Chicago house music. A professional actress and dancer for most of her life, she has her own dance company, Fivestarboogie Productions. She belongs to three different DJ crews: the Untouchables, with Farley "Jackmaster Funk," Paul Johnson, and Gene Hunt; 3 Degrees Global; and the Strictly 90s Crew. She has played and had residencies in the Philippines, all over Asia, and in the US. In Chicago, she has had residences at Smartbar, Crocodile, Boom Room, Grandbar, Evil Olive, Hydrate, Circuit, and many others.

MLH: You've done so much, I'm not sure how to categorize where you fit. You're an originator, an innovator, and a guardian of the flame.

Czboogie: Thank you for not doing the usual. The dancers are more important than the DJ sometimes.

MLH: I want to focus on house music as a whole community. Right, so not just the DJs and the producers, they're important, but house music itself, to me, is a character in the whole thing. The music itself, and the dancers and the crowds and everyone in it. I want to focus on that and also talk about the women. I'm excited to talk to you. Tell me about your first experience with house music and where you were, who you were with. What did it make you feel? Oh, my god! You've really got a disco ball in your living room! [Our interview was via Zoom.]

Czboogie: I know, right? But when I do the videos, the angles, it looks more impressive. Anyway, house music. So, I grew up in the Philippines. I grew up there my whole life.

MLH: Where in the Philippines?

Czboogie: Manila, Philippines. My mom's Filipino. My dad is East Indian. We have a disco in our house. We had a little disco, and my mom would play disco. Not a disco open to the public. A room that has all these lights and mirrors. It looks like something from the seventies, and she would play disco all the time. So that was my first experience of house, pre-house.

Then I went to college at Northwestern, and I didn't hear any house there. It wasn't until my first clubs, Shelter and China Club. I used to go to the Black fraternity parties and then that's when I started hearing house. A DJ for those parties was a DJ named Kelly G. And now he's huge! He would take me around. He took me to China Club. He took me to Shelter. So that was my first experience of house. I loved it. You know, I'm a dancer, right?

MLH: And actress, model, influencer.

Czboogie: (Laughs modestly)

MLH: Well, you are. You're a producer, I mean you do it all.

Czboogie: I don't know if you ever heard of Joel Hall Dancers?

MLH: Yes!

Czboogie: I became a scholar there, and I actually danced for the company. He played all house music, girl! In his classes, he would play tapes of Darrell Woodson. He would just play mixtapes of house all the time. Everyone just got indoctrinated to house music. It was a mixture of my mom, disco in the Philippines, and then the Black fraternity parties at Northwestern, and then Joel Hall when I was dancing. Because I was there morning, noon, and night, and I just loved it. I was drawn to the female diva vocals, you know, very uplifting. The female voice uplifts my soul. Those screaming churchy vocals, I love that. So, yeah, that's it.

MLH: Oh wow, I love that. Can you expand on that a little bit more? What is it about the female vocals that drew you in?

Czboogie: That's why I love playing gay clubs, because there's something special. You know not everyone is attracted to vocal house. It reminds me of church. It reminds me of a diva. It's something that's just in your heart, that just speaks to you, like the vocal, that high-pitched voice that just takes you to a higher plane. That was ecstasy to me. Just the voice. That was my spirit, you know? And that's it, that's all I got.

Oh, I went to the Generator, right before it was the Mid—I would go there and get my little Bacardi and listen to Dana Powell. But I never went when it was the first location on Halstead. There was RednoFive.... Yeah, so many good clubs.

MLH: So, then how did you start DJing?

Czboogie: *5 Magazine* started in 2005.... A side note to all this is, all this time I was going to clubs, I didn't know anybody. I'd always go by myself or with my dancer friends, and I was blissfully unaware of who the DJ was. I was just, like, just let me dance.

It was in 2005, I started the magazine and I started interviewing all the DJs. I just wanted to learn how to DJ for technical purposes. I was so ashamed to ask because I thought people would think, "Oh, here comes another girl, wanting to learn how to DJ." My boyfriend at the time, Rees Urban, who is an amazing DJ and producer, was helping me with the magazine. He helped me get a lot of interviews with people because he knew everybody. I just asked him to teach me how to DJ and he did. We had Thursday nights (DJing) together at the old Betty's Blue Star Lounge, so I got to practice. I worked really hard. I get obsessed when I learn something, so I took it very seriously. Reese was making sure that I didn't suck because, you know...

MLH: Because you're on his ticket?

Czboogie: Right, exactly. So I was initially just curious to see what it was like. And it kind of just took off because, you know, I already had some connections.

MLH: Tell me about your connection with Andre Hatchett. Are you his protégé? Did you learn from him? After Ron Hardy, he's my all-time favorite DJ. Back in the day, if Andre Hatchett was spinning at a party, I'd break my neck to be there. I can hear it in the way you play. It's a lineage for me, in terms of your heart, and I can hear it in the way you choose music, in the way you move the crowd, in the way that you're feeling it.

Do you play for the crowds, or do you play for yourself? I feel like you really play for yourself, but that it is an extension of us, the crowd. I feel that connection, and there is something very special about that.

Czboogie: Well, with Andre, when I was in the early years of *5 Mag*, I kind of stuck more to the South Side. I kind of stuck to the more old-school DJs in the beginning. I used to follow him around. I used to go hear him play at the Dating Game on Sixty-Seventh Street, and then we became good buddies, drinking beer, making food. I probably absorbed it. He never said, "This is what you do," but I absorbed so much from him, and I've interviewed him so many times that I'm sure I'm his protégé that way.

MLH: Yeah, you're carrying on his lineage.

Czboogie: I love it, and that makes me so happy, so flattering. Andre, I love me some Andre. But I guess, you know, when you watch a DJ so many times, they kind of are your teachers, right? You know you're just observing all the time and Andre, I've seen him so many times and learned so many lessons from him, you know?

MLH: Yeah, so it seemed like you really had a natural proclivity. As a creative person, it seems like you naturally really just picked it up. Because some people can do it or see it and not pick it up.

Czboogie: Oh, well, thank you. That's so nice of you. Thanks. I do think maybe because I started out as a dancer, and I think maybe that helps. As a dancer in the club, I was observing for a long time. I think if you started out as a DJ, from the beginning, you're a little bit detached. I was that girl rolling around on the floor for years and years and years and didn't know anybody, and maybe that helps me DJ a different way than someone who started out DJing at eleven years old. You're informed differently. You know what you like to hear. You know what you like to dance to. I'm just guessing maybe that is the difference, my background.

MLH: That's a question I had. As an actress and as a dancer, how has that informed how you play?

Czboogie: You know, I don't play as crazy and as larger-than-life when I'm behind the decks. I keep it cool, honey. (Laughs.) I don't understand when people are playing and they go crazy. I don't understand how people do that. I'm more drawn to DJs that are kind of cool, calm, and collected and let the music speak.

MLH: So as a dancer and actress, as a creative, not in terms of the theatrical of how you look or how people view you, but how and what you play? With the choices of music that you play, or how you bring us in and bring us out?

Czboogie: Well, if you hear any of my sets, you know that I love anything Frankie. I never got to hear Ron Hardy. I'm so drawn to Frankie Knuckles. I love big sounds. I love orchestrations like big horn sections, big pianos. In that way, if that's what you mean, I like very Broadway. I'm kind of drawn to that. I can never be, I'm not a minimal person, just beats.

MLH: Yeah, because as a dancer, you know what you want to hear, and so that has to influence the kinds of the music that you actually choose to play.

Czboogie: Yeah, big, I love big. I love big sounds, orchestrations, stuff with flair, the theatrics, you know, drama, baby.

MLH: What were their challenges for you as a female DJ or as a woman of color? Were there challenges? Were there advantages?

Czboogie: There never was. I found it was an advantage because you're kind of the novelty. Probably not anymore, but I think we have an advantage if you're a female DJ.

As a woman of color, I never felt any kind of disadvantage, but where I did feel a disadvantage was when I started DJing. That's why I was kind of like, "Don't tell anyone I'm a DJ. Just don't tell anyone I'm trying to learn how to DJ." I was a little bit embarrassed in the beginning because, at least at that time, I was already doing the magazine, already hosting lots of parties. I was already very active in the scene and I really felt it, especially from the men.

MLH: Yeah, other women have said similar things like that. That it is an advantage, at first it was a novelty, but then there's also a kind of old boys' club and they're kind of looking at you sideways, like, "Can you really DJ?"

Czboogie: I will tell you one thing that I have noticed, and I will stand by this. There is a little subtle thing with male DJs that I've seen toward all my sister DJs. I don't think I've seen one [a female DJ] that has ever done this. I am very respectful in terms of time. If I have to play from five to six and then the next person comes on from six to seven, I'm super nice, I'm almost pushed-over nice. I'll get off ten minutes before my set and let the person set up so they start right at six. Some people end their set at 6:00 or 6:05. But I've noticed with a lot of male DJs—sometimes, not all—they'll be like one more [song], or two more, or three more. And they like to do that with other DJs, but they'll flex and see how much they can kind of push you. There's like these little intimidation tactics that they'll do, or they'll leave you with like a thirty-second song to blend, so you're scrambling. It's subtle, but I've noticed with female DJs, they're very respectful of time and your space, and they'll explain the equipment to you. Because usually, the protocols are when you're about to get off, the next DJ gets on and you kind of explain the setup. They will say, "So this is where the lines are, the mixer's a little wonky, make sure this is that," you know. We kind of look out for each other. We do that for each other. It's not always like that with men. On the flip side, I just want to say, those are few and far between. Most times, men are so generous. It's just a personality thing.

MLH: And I think competitive. There wasn't as much competition between women as there is with the guy DJ, is that right?

Czboogie: Correct, correct.

MLH: So that's interesting, though, that *5 Magazine* came first and the DJing came later.

Czboogie: It was just like, "Hey, why don't we start this publication? Let's give it a shot." I literally did not know anybody, you know.

MLH: Wow, so you've really done a lot for the dance music community, not just in Chicago but I feel like globally now.

Czboogie: Aw, thank you!

MLH: Did it just start out as a labor of love then?

Czboogie: Yes, yes, yes. There was a crew of us. We had a small editorial team. My partner, he's my managing editor, Terry Matthew, who pretty much runs the magazine right now. In the last year, I've kind of taken a step back, just for now. I just did it for the love. I just thought it'd be cool. There really was no publication that was dedicated exclusively to house music. You had *Mix Mag*, you had maybe one other, *DJ Mag*, but it was all the genres. I just wanted to do house and really focus on Chicago house.

MLH: That's amazing. I feel like it's really done a lot.

Czboogie: Thank you.

MLH: There are so many things I want to ask you. I guess moving from that, can you talk about your involvement with 3 Degrees? How did that really get started and what was your involvement in it?

Czboogie: I used to go to 3 Degrees parties on Wednesdays. I didn't know anybody. I followed them and then the magazine came along. Fast-forward ahead, I think it might have been 2014 or something—they had a residency at Primary nightclub. They were doing Wednesdays there, and I was going to be a guest. DJ Jeremiah Seraphine, he's the one who started 3 Degrees. They asked me to DJ, and at the time, the Philippines had a typhoon, a very bad typhoon, so I asked if we could make it a benefit and give the proceeds, and they said, "Sure," so I played. Then that night, Jeremiah kind of vaguely said something about me joining them, and I didn't understand what that was. I still didn't know what it was five years later, and they were always asking, "Do you want to play with us?" So now, six years later, I think I realized that I am part of 3 Degrees. I played with them everywhere. There's been so many. We were at Primary. We were at Betty's Blue Star Lounge, Grand Bar. It's so funny. On a side note, I'm actually in three DJ crews. I'm in the Strictly 90s crew, which is John Simmons and Gant-Man [Gant Garrard]. Strictly 90s is a crew where we go around and play different nineties house music at different clubs, and it's always been a big hit because a lot of our audience loves nineties. I was also in the Untouchables, and that was Farley ["Jackmaster" Funk] Keith, Paul Johnson, Gene Hunt, Box, and Craig Alexander.

But 3 Degrees, it was an honor to be with them. They had their heyday, I think, more like in the early 2000s. It was such a strong community. There's such a strong community, and every DJ is so different, and I really love being a part of it. People moved and everyone's kind of doing their own thing. Sometimes we still do parties, but I miss everybody, you know?

MLH: Yeah, because now it's truly global. San Francisco, Singapore. I would love to see more events happening and sort of bringing everyone out together. I wanted to ask what is it like, internationally, particularly in the Philippines or other places that you've played, as opposed to how it is in Chicago?

Czboogie: For the first five years when I went back to the Philippines, I got gigs there and my friends would look out for me. My Filipino friends would say, "You could play here, here, or here, and there are people who love house music." My experience—there's always going to be people who love house music and a small scene in every country. I didn't meet any female DJs.

MLH: What do you want people to know about you and your role in the house music community?

Czboogie: I think I've done every facet of life in the house world. You know, everyone does at some point. I started out as a dancer, like most people do. Literally dancing at the club, in the circle, just dancing up a storm. And then the magazine happened. Then I became a publisher, and I became someone who disseminates information. Really my goal was to write about all the different people in house, and when the magazine started, we would talk about door people. We would talk about the bar people. We would talk about coat check people, the dancers. It's really just shining a light and making it a thing about all of house music, as opposed to just about the general clubs, like other magazines did.

Then I became a DJ, and that kind of just took control. I would host a lot of parties for people because I was super social. So, dancer, magazine publisher, host, and then DJ. But I think a lot of people, to really be in the community, I think you end up becoming a little bit of everything. A person who was at parties at one time starts promoting or DJing. You dabble. I guess I just want people to know I really, really love the scene. I really respect the scene.

I had a lot of challenges in the beginning because I wasn't from Chicago. They're like, "Who's this Filipino girl?" And I don't blame them. But my intentions were pure and it was never to take advantage of it. I loved house so much that I was like, "Whoa, let's write about it," you know? I guess that's what I want people to know.

MLH: Yeah, and I think people saw that, because we are very tribal in Chicago. We're very much about "Where you from?" But also, people see your sincerity, and they see that you are genuine, see you are trying to be part of the community, as opposed to taking from the community. Then I think Chicago is very generally loving and welcoming.

Czboogie: Listen, that's one of my favorite parts. Like I said in the beginning when I would only go to South Side parties, I'd be like, "Man, this is the shit!" Just going to someone's house, but everyone's kind. It was an older crowd. They're just warmer, and then I would bring all kinds of white people with me, you know? People would be so friendly. It's really different. I really am drawn to the South Side.

I also wanted to say was, like, a lot of people that are not from Chicago, I feel like almost love Chicago more than Chicago loves Chicago.

MLH: Oh, talk about that.

Czboogie: Just the passion I see. Because we hear from so many different people through the magazine. People from France or Japan, and just their passion for Chicago house is so palpable. They just really love Chicago house. They're big fans. Chicago DJs often say you could go overseas and say you're a Chicago DJ and they're just in awe of you. They have a really, really big respect, and I don't think we should underestimate that.

MLH: That's great, thank you for that.

THE MAYOR OF HYDE PARK: A CONVERSATION WITH MARIO SMITH

Mario Smith has been dubbed "the Mayor of Hyde Park." He is a poet, educator, activist, radio host of the Lumpen Radio Show, *News from the*

Service Entrance, WLPN, Chicago, and host of the Silver Room podcast, *Randomly Selected*. For over twenty years, Mario has been the voice of the community, to the community. He is featured in David Weathersby's new documentary, *It's Different in Chicago*, about the history of house and hip-hop music in the city.

MLH: I've heard they call you "the Mayor of High Park," but you are to me "the People's Mayor" because you are just everywhere. Every place I've ever been, you are always there: North Side, South Side, West Side, wherever.

MS: I don't know about all that, but I appreciate it.

MLH: You are a poet, educator, activist, podcast host, radio host, always doing a lot of stuff for a long time. Mario, I can't remember when I met you. Maybe it was during Lit-Ex time in the nineties?

MS: Yeah, I was thinking about that the other day. How long have I known this woman? I could only go up to maybe Spices?

MLH: What year was that? 1990?

MS: When I came back to Chicago, it was like '92.

MLH: Okay, '92, which is a long time now. So, tell me about your first experience with house music. Where were you? Who was with you? What did it make you feel?

MS: I guess it would have been one of the last parties Ron Hardy threw before he passed away, at the Music Box. I had been going with a much older woman. I'd been going with a friend of mine's sister. He has no idea. I'm not gonna say his name. Still to this day, he has no idea that me and his sister used to go out.

MLH: How did you pull that off?

MS: I have no idea. I was young and did not have a plan. She would take me to the Music Box. I was a kid. My first experience was like, "Whoa!" I mean, I saw a lot of stuff. The most memorable thing was a night that I went there with a bunch of friends of mine from Hyde Park Career Academy. I went to CVS [Chicago Vocational High School].

One of my friends and his girlfriend got into a fight, and I guess he drove her home. We were all stuck at the Music Box, and it was like seven or eight in the morning, or something like that, and our ride was gone. We didn't have cell phones, and somebody had to find a pay phone and call him. We barely caught up with him. He was coming back to get us.

We knocked on the door because we can't be out there. We don't want to go to jail for curfew. We couldn't be on Lower Wacker Drive because it was kind of shady down there, you know? So, we knock on the door, bang, bang, bang. And then the door opens up, Ron Hardy sticks his head out. As soon as sees us, he closes the door. Then he opens it up again and says, "What do y'all want?" We said, "Man, we're stuck. We're waiting on a ride. We got nowhere to go." Then he opened up the door to play for us for another hour and a half.

MLH: Oh wow!

MS: So that's when I knew how house music worked. I knew it was a community and a family, and these were people who looked out for each other. It would be years before I figured out why that was and where the origins of that came from, but he made me and a bunch of kids safe. He was like, "Yeah, come in." Now, I knew who he was, but I had no idea that he was one of the greatest DJs ever, ever, ever. He played for us for about an hour and a half, and he kept playing. He kind of subtly was like, "I'm tired," and then we were like, "All right, we'll leave." But he was a very nice man. It was a beautiful thing.

MLH: He protected you.

MS: I'm going to say he was the only one there that was an adult. Everybody else was like seventeen, maybe eighteen years old or something. I don't think I realized how special that was until many, many years later. I knew it was a special thing because he didn't have to do it, but I did not know the gravity of the moment and why it was so dope that he did that for us. I wish I could have told him, given him a real proper thank you for that. I never had a chance to.

MLH: Well, that's what we're doing now.

MS: Definitely.

MLH: I feel like the house movement in Chicago, in particular, is, in a lot of ways, a continuation of the Black Arts Movement or a continuation of the Black Aesthetic. Do you feel that way and can you talk about that a little bit?

MS: I mean, the Black—house music, as I said in David's documentary, house music and hip-hop is about struggle. There was a voice, a certain voice. People after the disco era got exploited. They needed to be able to have someplace safe to go, to listen to the music they liked without being criticized or possibly hurt. These parties that developed, particularly in Chicago, were places where people could be themselves. Everybody, young people who were coming out, young artists that were going to these parties, that were coming out. Not just coming out and making an announcement that they were gay, I mean coming out period, just becoming adults and becoming artists. I think the term "coming out" is kind of not used properly, but in this context, there were people whose artistic lives were starting to develop, and the one place they could go, where they would not see criticism for what they were doing, or for how they felt sexually, or what kind of music they liked, was a house party. In the same vein, you could say that about hip-hop ciphers and events like with Duro, and what we were doing at the Lower Links $2 Hip-Hop Show. To be able to be yourself, and not be criticized for what you were doing—it was in the house music stuff that was really centered on music, culture, art, and expression. The sense of adventure of sneaking out of your house or not telling your parents where you would go. Staying out all night and well into the daytime, and then coming back home and acting like nothing had happened, when in reality in your head and your body—you saw it all happen.

So I think the Black Arts Movement, and that comparison with house music—it's not off at all. I think they both share a lot of that same energy, the idea of expression and the ability to be able to express yourself without feeling like you're gonna be criticized and, again, hurt. Because there were some people who like to take the violent end of things, and that didn't really happen with house music. Being in Chicago, there's always an element of danger involved. You just gotta keep your head on a swivel and know who you're with.

MLH: Can you talk about the intersection between house music and hip-hop in Chicago? Because really it was some of the same people, some of the same places.

MS: The first time I really saw that the thing was real, that kind of thing, was when I saw Common at Red Dog, at a house party. And he was jacking hard, I mean, I didn't know my man could dance like that. He was killing it.

MLH: Did you feel the division between house and hip-hop before?

MS: Absolutely. It was kind of like *West Side Story*, you know, where you had one faction of folks who were strictly house music and claimed they never listened to hip-hop. And you had another faction of folks who were hard-core hip-hop that claimed they never listened to house music. And here's Common, and he's at both, and he's at a point in his career where people are just really starting to catch on that he's a mega-talented dude. They see him at these house music parties, and it's a sense of relief almost for me because I'm like, "Oh, word. He's here, so it's okay if I'm here because I like hip-hop too." I really love both genres of music, so I'm seeing him getting it, and I think, "Okay, this is not a bad place to be." And that is when I knew, when I saw that man at Red Dog, that the music was the message. That's the part that brought everybody in, but to see a person like that, back in those days, made it cool to know that you could go to both. So that's when I started seeing people and seeing how those worlds started to actually be more together than I knew. I guess it was more of a separation for me because I was still trying to find my way. But once again, once I saw him at that joint, the first time I saw him at Red Dog and it was a legit house party, I was like, "Oh shit." He was getting down. I think a lot of things started to click for me in Wicker Park during that Lit-Ex era, when I thought, these things are closer than they are apart—and that faction started to come together.

After a while, you got people like Duane Powell, or people like Javon Jackson, people like Jesse De La Pena, who can play. They play music, but they don't distinguish the two, they just play it.

Think of throwing a set with a million house songs and a million hip-hop songs, and run those joints together and it was seamless. I think over time, this intersection of hip-hop and the intersection of house music started to form the superhighway, where it just all became really good music. The familiarity that people have with both genres. We started with rap music, and with house music, that intersection became a common thing that is real, and that's where we're at now. It's not a big deal to see me and Duane Powell play all house music or an all-Brazilian music thing. And then, while I'm there, he's playing, you know, a track from Public Enemy or something. It's no longer an anomaly. It's not weird. It's what it's supposed to be, which is good music being played. The hip-hop culture and the house music culture have way more similarities than people will admit. They all formed under those same tenets, including the sexuality. People do not want to talk about that at all, but you know what you see, and you hear what you hear, and you notice people are people. I think those stigmas are the reasons why these conversations are necessary because it shouldn't be a big deal anymore—it's 2022.

MLH: How did you experience house music on the South Side versus the North Side? Can you talk about the venues, the crowds? How was it different, or similar?

MS: I don't know because the house music culture was always part of everything in my experience, another one of those "aha moments"—I must have been in my freshman year, sophomore year—we would walk through the halls in between classes, you get four minutes, and during those four minutes, everybody would sing "Din Da Da" in the hallway. So now I want you to imagine, every period, especially when we saw somebody we knew, and they would start and everybody would sing it. I'm pretty sure we did it every period. Yeah, everybody singing "Din Da Da." Not a few people, not like fifty people. Every, damn, body. That was our jam.

I would be going to parties, around CVS [Chicago Vocational High School], on Seventy-Fifth and Exchange, down the street from my house. That was a party I could actually go to and not get in trouble for. Seventy-Fifth was a lot cooler than it is now.

I don't want to fake like I was at all these parties because my family wasn't having that, but I definitely knew the minimum things happening, and I went to a bunch of those. I went to a house party once in the hundreds that almost turned into something else, with a girl I was seeing. I was totally unprepared for all the gangbanging that was at this one particular house party, so I had to finagle my way out.

They thought I was in a gang and I wasn't. I got out of there.

I went to mostly your downtown stuff, the Playground, the Music Box, and things like that. I guess it was more on the South Side when I was little, because we would only go as far as the South Loop. Me getting indoctrinated into the Wicker Park stuff happened well after all that.

MLH: How are the literary and poetry scenes in Chicago influenced and affected by house music and the house music community?

MS: I think it's a direct effect, depending on who the poet is. I think poets, and folks who are more charged by rap music—I think all those same folks would find a way to be at a house party because they didn't have to think about that structure of what rap is. Rap is a lot of things, including a lot of work. A lot of work. It's not as easy at a hip-hop show. At a rap show, you are kind of observing the room, checking for talents, to see if people are side-eyeing you. I'm trying to listen, trying to get that cadence and stuff. And I don't want to generalize it because I'm sure there are some folks who are influenced by disco music. I think it is because of the, I don't want to say carefree, but because there aren't so many restrictions, and it's not so much work. To say, "I'm not going to think about any of this shit. I'm going to release. I'm going to dance. I want to have a good time. I'm going to see my friends. We're going to drink and talk shit and have fun and listen to some amazing music and keep it moving."

MLH: What do you see happening with the new underground scene or the younger folks? What's happening in Chicago now?

MS: It's good for them to use their authentic voice, and they're doing that right now. They're trying to figure out their voice. I think the music scene in Chicago is in great shape. There are a lot of great artists here who play music, who dance, who do their thing and do it really, really well.

I don't see there being a shortage of talented young people in our city. I think the problem is them being able to get that music played on terrestrial radio. That is a problem. I think because they don't need terrestrial radio, it is also a problem. As a society, we are people who used to turn on the radio to listen to get information. I turn on the radio, and I don't hear music that speaks to my spirit. I don't listen to the radio, and this is someone that's been on the radio for a while—right, twenty years now in various forms.

I don't listen to the radio. I listen to like Sirius XM or I play an album.

Radio stations like WGCI are programmed by somebody that doesn't understand the historical nature of music in Chicago. It is hard to program for the city because you're playing music that you think people like. And in turn, because they hear it so much, they begin to say, "I must like this." It's psychological warfare.

If I programmed WGCI for a month, I could change the way people listen to music in Chicago, and that's not me bragging. That's just that same psychological warfare, flipped. If I'm programming Stevie Wonder on WGCI and making people listen to Marvin Gaye, I'm programming music that changes people's attitudes and raises the vibration and gives them things to think about as opposed to reacting to things.

If [music] makes you want to shoot somebody instead of making you figure out, "How can I be more of a person that loves people because of the music I'm listening to?" that changes the vibration in the city. That changes things. When WGCI is being the soundtrack to death, it's hard to listen to, because you know what that is, and you know what it means. This isn't a slight to any of my friends that work for WGCI, and I have several. It must be hard, because you have to play music that you don't even listen to. We've got artists in Chicago who are amazingly dope that can't get played on stations like WGCI. They just can't. They make music for Black people and those people who love.

The music that is part of the soundtrack of our death is getting played twenty-four hours a day. It's troubling. So I think the reason why these young people are like, "Well, I don't need the radio" is because radio don't need them right now. And they're not changing their position either. They're going to continue to play that shit because it makes money, and people's deaths have always made money. I mean what else is it? What's happening? I don't like it.

I would love to work with WGCI, bad. I have wanted to be able to give those call letters out. I've been wanting to do that my whole career, but there's no way in hell they're going to have me because I'm not gonna play what they tell me to play.

MLH: And you're going to speak the truth in a way that they can't deal with.

MS: I'm so happy that the path I've taken has led me to where I am. But if they ever offered me a job and would let me play what I want to play on WGCI, I would go in a second, because I know how many people a station like that reaches. Unfortunately, they are consumed with being capitalist when it comes to the death of Black people. They don't give a shit, and their not giving a shit is the reason why a lot of this is happening. They continue to be the drumbeat of death, and as long as they're doing that, and making money doing it, it's never going to change. It just isn't, so when these young artists that are here, making good music, or making money and being able to survive without the radio, considering how the radio is, I applaud them for that.

They are being heard now online, at parties, and at certain music venues that have the balls to let them open up for a big act. Underground. I think it all goes back to the DJ. Thank God for Bandcamp because you can find artists that way. I'm on SoundCloud. Those entities address the needs and give those people that movement of life. I'm not saying that the only avenue is the radio, but I'm talking about in Chicago, Illinois. If they could get those songs, if they could get these artists who I know are brilliant, I know people here would love them. I know they would. And the programming at favorite radio stations reflects the sound of the city.

MLH: How has house music healed you personally or how has it influenced your work as a writer and producer?

MS: It has made me one. It's like yesterday, on the Lumpen Radio show, I played "Way Back When" by Brenda Russell because I'm hearing it more now at house parties and at events that people DJ. I think what house music, what disco music does, it makes me a quasi-researcher. I go back to listen to the original version of that song. I think I'm being an attentive listener.

It just gives me more things to learn about. I don't know how much it affects me when it comes to my writing. I think it affects more in just my general every day, and how I go about things.

How music makes me feel personally? House music is like a big sample library, I can go back and listen to the samples or go back and listen to the originals from the samples.

MLH: It's like an education?

MS: Right, that's exactly what it is. House music is an education. That's it. House music is an education.

That's how you form these relationships and that's how you get these lifelong friendships. It's all off of the music. It's like a big warm fireplace. Everybody gets around these fireplaces. Everybody goes to these house music parties. There's nothing like it. I've seen it a million times, particularly the Silver Room Block Party when Ron Trent starts playing. People, I don't care where they were, they find that stage, and they listen to Ron and he does it. He does the job.

MLH: Eric Williams is one of those culture bearers.

MS: There's nothing like knowing people who get it. And I've worked for Eric. Before I started working for him, I was working with him to make sure that people understood that this was part of our culture. We have to keep it and we've got to maintain it. He's an amazing dude, and he's done a wonderful job. And the people who work with him are amazing too. And again, the affirmation that I'll call him Dr. Ron Trent is the man. People like that and Duane Powell, Steve Hurley, and Lori Branch, Heather, and DJ Lady D. I mean, all these folks—they are the epitome of physician, heal thyself. They do that. They get you back to your right self.

MLH: How are you literally or figuratively writing the new Black template? How do you see that?

MS: I guess the way I'm writing it now is with my voice. I'm not really writing poems like I used to.

I remember something Chuck D said to me a long time ago when I interviewed him, and I asked him, "Where have y'all been? We need you?" He was looking down and said, "Sometimes you have to sit back and observe." And he went back to whatever he was doing. I heard him and felt that. Right now I think, although I still write poems and stuff, I think I'm doing more with my voice by being on the radio and doing the podcasts and trying to lend my voice to things. I'm a poet but focusing on being a better radio personality.

MLH: I just wanted to say how much I honor, love, and respect you, and I appreciate your participation in this project.

ALL THE BLK, ALL THE BEAUTY, ALL THE SOUL: A CONVERSATION WITH AVERY R. YOUNG

Avery R. Young is a West Side native. On April 24, 2023, Mayor Lori Lightfoot named him the inaugural Chicago poet laureate. He is an interdisciplinary writer, performer, composer, producer, visual artist, and activist. He personifies music. The way he uses language, the cadence of his voice, the way he tells a story, is soulful and melodious. It was my hope to capture as much of the essence of our conversation as possible. If you haven't heard Avery read or sing, or if you haven't experienced his art, please do so. You can watch and listen to his albums, *booker t. soltreyne* and *tubman*, and (my jam), "Ham Sammich(is)," on YouTube. You can find his most recent book, *neckbone: visual verses*, from Northwestern University Press.

MLH: Thank you so much for being a part of this project. You fit in at least three of the different categories. You are an Originator and Innovator and a Guardian of the Flame. You represent soul, gospel, rhythm and blues, and house music.

ARY: To me, house is a very different thing, because when most people are talking about house and the tradition of house in Chicago, they're talking about things that happened in the eighties, specifically parties that happened in the eighties. I'm not party "able" until 1994, just because of my age. I stayed off of North Avenue and Central. I grew up right near DaVinci Manor. DaVinci Manor was right down the street from me, where a lot of house parties happened. So when I was a kid, and we're going to the 7-Eleven, I would see the high school kids and grown-ups lined up to go into the party. There would be people hanging out in the White Castle across the street. All of this stuff that's happening all around me, so I was definitely *interested.* I was like, "Ooo, I'm going there."

MLH: What was your first experience of house music? When was it? Where was it? What did it make you feel?

ARY: Okay, so this is another thing about house music and me—I think of house music in everything, depending on what genre of house music you're talking about. My first experience of house music is at the crib.

MLH: Okay, talk about that.

ARY: As I began to party, go to house parties, they would be playing all the records my cousins, my big cousins, would be playin', all while I was little. They would be playin' the music that my uncle, all of them were into. The stuff that you heard on the radio. Those were the cuts.

So in my molecular memory, my first experiences with house music is in the context of growing up Black—Black in Chicago—in a very religious house. Or a house that was headed by a very religious person, which then just breeded the idea that her children would listen to the most freaky, debaucherous shit they could listen to. So in the context of molecular memory, my first experience of house music is as a child, listening. Culture-wise, in the context of culture, the first time I went to a quote-unquote house party, understood house music, was fourteen years old and in high school, because they were playing what we all would know and understand to be house music.

I grew up out West, on North Avenue and Central where, at the time, you had the Starter jackets and the straight-lined jeans, and the music of that neighborhood. You had a mix of blues, 'cause there were the taverns, and there are still taverns around that neighborhood that play the down-home blues.

MLH: The nasty blues.

ARY: Right. The nasty blues. And then you have the storefront churches, all on that strip. That's where the music, the gospel music, is coming out [onto the street]. What's coming out of the radios is more urbanized, what has become a more urban WGCI, V103—you know, shit Black folks listen to . . . whatever people were listening to in their homes, which has always been a mixture of R and B, soul, and gospel.

In my house, I tell the people, that's where I get the term "Sunday Morning Juke Joint," because my house, it was gospel music coming from Big Mama, and in the basement, it was all kinds of Millie Jackson. Mahalia Jackson is what my Big Mama was playing. Millie Jackson is what my uncles and them were playing. So I had all of this. My cousins and her kids would be playing Con Funk Shun and Jimi Hendrix. So all of this music, this Black music, I was always entrenched in. When I went to the house parties and heard the quote-unquote old-school cuts, the old disco cuts—where the term "house" comes from, the tracks that were played at the Warehouse, and all the tracks that people are building on, and the different producers are working on and building on—all of that happens when I'm around thirteen or fourteen. When I start going to parties, I got more and more into the house culture. As I become an older teen, I decide I can have a foolproof plan of how I can be outside all night and not get caught by Big Mama. So when I had that all figured out, now you're talking about going to Medusa's, going to the Factory, the Power Plant. All of that stuff happened in my later teens, once I had the foolproof plan.

MLH: Yeah, because you had to have a plan. You had to be staying at somebody's house or something because the parties didn't even get going good until two o'clock in the morning.

ARY: My plan was real simple. I went to bed.

MLH: That worked?

ARY: Oh, it worked thoroughly. I went to bed. See, what happened was, I would go to bed at like ten. Then she'd go to bed.

MLH: Okay, so she's not getting up to check on you?

ARY: No. No. No. No. No. None of that. None of that. None of that, which is wild style. I don't think she thought she would have to check on me at night, because her thing was, "Ole' man done already went to bed." It all worked in my favor. My nickname from her was Ole' Man because she'd say, "He go to bed like he old. Whatever it is, he's gonna be in bed by ten." That she could bank on. So, I'd just lay in bed and wait until about eleven thirty.

MLH: Now, did you go out the front door, back door, or window? How'd you get out?

ARY: We had a basement. I had the basement. I went out the front door. If I went back door, I would have got caught, because her bedroom was near the back door. So for me to come up the stairs from the basement and leave out the back door totally would have shut that down. I was able to walk out the front door. Now what happened was, I figured that I could not come to the house at two or three o'clock in the morning—there wasn't no way that was gonna happen—so I would stay out until morning, ring the doorbell, and would act like I forgot my keys. She would be like, "Boy, you would lose yo head if you could screw if off." The funny part is, I told her this when I was in my thirties, when we were lollygagging a few years ago and all that good stuff. She would bring it up. "Avery went to bed at ten. With these girls, I would have to fuss with them." And I just started laughing and told her what I would do. She was bewildered and hurt.

MLH: I can't believe you told her. My grandmother never knew. She would have whooped my ass at fifty if she knew.

ARY: Her reaction to it was, like, I should have never told her, but I figured, at the time, she knew. I was damn near thirty years old. She said, "All kinds of things could have happened to you." And then I had to explain to her, "No. Actually no." Then I'd have to explain to her the culture.

You know, you're talking about people going somewhere to dance, and you are in a warehouse, you're in a loft, you're in a club. Ain't no window to tell you that it's ten in the morning when you walk out. When you walk out, the sun is shining. You've been jackin' all night. Or you went to the Golden Nuggets or sat up and ate at IHOP being a loud, wild teenager at a twenty-four-hour table.

So time is elapsed. And you know, to me, that's the best party, when the time has elapsed. When I say time elapsed, I mean not just from the time you go into a place and out of the place. It has everything to do with the way in which the music is being blended. You know, you're just transfixed in a space where time isn't about three thirty or four thirty. Time is about energy.

The time I spend in jackin'. The time I spend dippin' in front of a person, in front of a friend, the shit is butter.

And I also associate, since a lot of my work as an artist is about that space of praise and liberation, not necessarily tied to any dogma or religious joint but just the act of moving a body that is Black.

My experience with house music, with house parties, is my thesis, is in support of my thesis that the most revolutionary, liberating thing we get to do is have access to our body. Because when Black folks—or with the indentured servants and enslaved Black folks—that's what made them slaves, their access to their body, the agency of their body.

Anything that you can do that is an agency of the body, is liberating, is anti-whatever this other shit is. That is all the way to fucking, to singing, to speaking on what you want to speak, what you want to say, them field hollers, them blues, and dancing.

MLH: Right. Because it was all part of our indigenous, religious experience.

ARY: Right, and because those three things are so associated with the ritual of transformation and connection with the spiritual world, house music and Sunday morning church is the same thing. It's the same space. It's the same space.

You know, sometimes you can't tell really religious people that, and sometimes you can't tell that to really nonreligious people, but it is worship. It is worship. It's not worship in the sense of you praising a god in the context of a colonized religion, but it is praise, and once you are being, you're demonstrating your closeness to God or a god. Because you're in a space where you're magical. You're in a space in which you are defying the thing that binds you.

It is all supposed to be breaking the shackles of what binds you so that you can be liberated enough to understand how to be humane to other humans, your extension of your advantage, which hasn't really got shit to do with magic Catholic or Muslim or Baptist. But the whole point of religion to me is, how do I treat somebody who ain't me?

Not that everything or every experience has to be a good one, because that's what the whole crucifix is about—the idea that there's no divinity without suffrage. I don't necessarily think we have to spend more time suffering. (Laughs.)

Y'all do understand that cross part was only one part, right? He wasn't thirty-three years on the cross. Just his last three days. Just his last three days on earth.

But I get it, I get the idea of the linkage between suffrage and divinity. But I also understand and honor those moments in which I'm around and in spaces with young queer or queer-friendly folk who are in a space where we are energy.

And the adjectives that usually divided outside of this party are the exact adjectives that unite us inside that energy.

There is no house music without a queer Black body. There is no house without the cis Black woman, the Black woman's body. There is no house music without the trans body.

There is no House music without these adjectives, because these adjectives who created it—who built the culture, who cultivated, who could cultivate a culture, who do the parties, who made the music—is all of this.

All of those adjectives are needed and bring forth that energy because those songs, those parties that they create, so that they can be placed in a space called community.

MLH: Well, that's the book right there.

ARY: What we mean when we say "community," ultimately, we mean a safe space to exist. Like I'm not coming to a house party and getting gay-bashed. I'm not coming to the house party and getting strung up on the tree.

It's not to say that there was not harm or danger in going to a house party. Because there were harm and dangers in the exploitations of body and power. I never experienced anything like that, but I know of people who have and people who would. With that being said, there was nothing I had to fear about the energy. There may have been things I needed to have been cognizant of, of another person. My West Side perihelial.

MLH: Right. Head on a swivel.

ARY: My West Side perihelial stays on, right. But there is nothing of the (negative) energy. "Yea, though I walk through the valley of the shadow of death, I fear no evil." Right.

MLH: "For thou art with me."

ARY: "For thou art with me. Thy rod and thy staff comfort me." It's like we're in a space where you have to fear no evil. And these places, some people remember, where the Warehouse was. Some people remember where some of these clubs we were going to, where Red Dog was.

MLH: Where the Music Box was, was a very scary place, at Lower Wacker Drive.

ARY: Right. Some people know these places.

MLH: Yeah, right. Red Dog, that was a stroll, right on North Avenue. Double Door was a hillbilly, country, gay bar, drug-dealing, stroll situation [before it became Double Door].

ARY: Right! And before it became Wicker Park, it was "Wicked!" That wasn't nothing nice. House music also helped transform those spaces, right? Because it was a different energy popping off in those spaces. A lot of times, it was like, "Oh wait, hold up, there can be some form of renewal in this space." So the development comes in the context of real estate that pushed a lot of those parties to another venue.

House music in Chicago is a very deep dive. That's not because of the lack of language to use or access, but it's because it actually is so much. There's so much that comes with the house music culture in Chicago. Because in Chicago, real estate is a very political thing. And because in Chicago, real estate and the spaces are very political and segregated. All of that informs the way everybody does shit.

MLH: That's right. That's my next question. How was your experience of house music different on the South Side versus the North Side versus the West Side? What did those experiences look like for you?

ARY: Taking a cab from the West Side, taking a cab up North, ain't no problem. Taking a cab back to the West Side, that's a problem. It's a whole motherfuckin' problem.

I can't be who I am today without being a creative. Because I am a creative, it was a necessity for me to travel south, west, north because that's where the poetry reading was, that's where whatever I gotta do, I gotta be over there. And I know people to this day, they only go to party at Reynold's because it's south. They ain't going up north, they ain't going out west, they going to Reynold's or somewhere south.

So for me, as a person who travels all throughout the city of Chicago simply because I just had to, because of what I do in life, the difference is just what my body needs and also who I am, as far as adjectives, my qualifiers. As a queer man, my queerness felt safer up North but not my Blackness. I'm on the South Side, my Blackness is all right, my queerness is like, "What the fuck?" (Jokingly looks around, scared and suspicious). On the West Side, it's like, "We don't give no fuck. They gon' learn today!" I know you know this about me, I ain't got no victim shit in me at all.

MLH: Right.

ARY: And I figured my job as a human being is to transform a space. Wherever my feet (hits the table three times, indicating hitting the ground), I'm supposed to be there. If my feet touch something and it don't feel right, I bounce. I don't force the shit. If the party's bunk, the people bunk, I'm out. Again, that is about a party being a space of community.

Up North, South, and West Side of Chicago, you get into very different communities when you talk about where you can go and get house music.

Case in point, the house music they're playing at Roscoe's on a Monday night ain't the house music you gon' hear at Reynold's on a Tuesday night because the audience—the premiere audience of it—are two different people. Folks at Roscoe's, I call "the Uncolas."

MLH: Ah, right. I know what you're talking about.

ARY: They dance like this (moves his hand straight up and down).

MLH: And if you were Brown and could even get into Roscoe's, right?

ARY: Right. And you can't be up in there without having to necessarily assimilate, right? That's why Rialto's was Rialto's.

So those people at Roscoe's, they're doing this, they dance like this (hand and arm moving straight up and down) and you can dance like that to this (mouthing the beat of a more techno house song): Dun dun dun, dunt dunt dunt, dun dun dun. You can do that there. But you go to boogie on that South Side, and you're dancing like this (motions his hand side to side in a wave pattern, indicating a more nuanced form of dancing, rather than a straight up-and-down basic beat kind of dancing).

You're dancing different. You're moving different, so the DJ is going to spin something different. The DJ is going to curate. I don't say that they spin. The DJ is a curator of energy, which is a powerful fucking thing.

MLH: Speak on it!

ARY: Let's get into that! Some people, when they are curating energy, will have you caught, the fuck, up!

MLH: Lost in it.

ARY: To a point in which you have to ground yourself, gather yourself, or the shit is over because you don't know where the fuck you've been.

MLH: Right, right. I dance with my eyes closed and that does happen. I'll be dancing and when I open them, I'm over on the other side of the room.

ARY: Right. And you don't know how. You know when you started, you were here. When you open your eyes, you don't know how you got all the way over there.

MLH: Right.

ARY: There's nothing in your conscious mind that recalls your journey from this end of the room to that end of the room. Or from your dry shirt to your drenched shirt. There's nothing in your conscious mind that can make markers to how that happened, outside of, "I'm at a party and I'm dancing." The heat is on "Middle Passage." We packed up in here, feet to head, head to foot.

MLH: Right. Butt to butt, booty to booty.

ARY: Right. We in here. And I always bring this back to: we are safe and we're amongst the community. Like I said, there's a very clear energy in a space that doesn't allow a Black or Brown body in it. Or doesn't allow a Black or Brown human, because them white folk are dancing to Black and Brown music. That, "Dun dun, dun dun dun, dunt" ain't made by other Uncolas. That shit is Gloria Gaynor, that shit is Sound of Philadelphia.

MLH: Donna Summer, Teddy Pendergrass . . .

ARY: That shit that they do is all informed by what Black and Brown people have given this culture. What they've given to the American songbook, plenty times, at the expense of their own back. White people get so mad at Black and Brown folks winning that they destroyed records at a ballpark in Chicago.

MLH: Right, right.

ARY: So let's talk about that. The racial climate of the eighties, at the time when this shit [house music] is being cultivated, that "Disco Sucks" shit is just a few years before. Just a few years. In Chicago, and Comiskey Park, which I believe is now US Cellular Field—to even understand, down the street from Comiskey Park ain't nothin' but Black folks. All of that happened in the midst of Black bodies.

MLH: They were burning Black bodies in effigy, basically, right? That's how I saw it.

ARY: Right. That's what that was. They were mad that their rock heroes were now making disco music, reluctantly. Okay, so now I'm about to get in trouble. People love them some Rod Stewart and some David Bowie, but them motherfuckas shitted on Black folks.

Them motherfuckas shitted on Black folks when the eighties came. When '85, '86 came, and they had to go back to their rock roots, and all that shit Nile Rodgers did for all them motherfuckas, they shitted on all that. "Fame" [by David Bowie] and all that shit we partied to, they shitted on all that music when they had to get back to rock and roll. And the craziest, most ignorant shit about all that is, rock and roll is us too, motherfuckas.

MLH: Hello! Right. And they've tricked Black people into thinking that it was white music, to where they had them looking at you like, "Why you listening to all that white music?" And I'm like, "Hello, Little Richard. Hello, Chuck Berry. Hello, Big Mama Thornton that Elvis stole from."

ARY: Right, and this is the thing, I'm a nerd and a creative, right? So there's a lot of history and research I go into a space with that most people just don't, because it ain't all about that. A lot of times for people, it's about a feeling. "I want to feel good and that party is where it's at, so I'm about to go up in here and feel good." I understand the danger and problem attached to Elvis. Elvis Presley is giving "white purity" a hard-ass time. Elvis Presley is moving like a poor white man, which is what he was. He grew up dirt poor in the American South and spent a considerable amount of time during his impressionable psychological development amongst Black folk. During the ages in which his social development and all that is starting to form, that happened around Black folk, which a lot of people don't understand.

Now he out here, jumping and gyrating like a nigga, getting these white girls into a fever pitch. And they screaming at him, like they screaming at Bo Diddley and all the other rock and rollers. Big Mama Thornton, wink, wink. And that kicks off the idea that, "Hey, we can make money." Elvis kicks off this idea that white people can do what we do. And to this day, white people love to show Black people that they can bounce and move and holler to the moon like we do. But I'm like, "You can't, because of all the issues associated with the shit you put Black folk through. You don't go through it." We may meet each other on economic planes, but you've created systems in which other additives separate us.

There's a difference between a Black man who made $20,000 and the white man who makes $20,000, and that difference is usually associated with that Black man's skin color.

It is this system, which they created, this is the system which then informs the music that a Muddy Waters makes. It is the music that that informs what Nile Rodgers is gonna make. Because now Rodgers is scoring Studio 54. That Chic, that's what they're doing up in Studio 54. They're playing the Chic's shit.

MLH: And then further on, informing new wave with Duran Duran and all of those other folks. Everything, right?

ARY: Everything. I was just having a conversation about Chaka Khan's "I Feel for You."

MLH: Which is a Prince song.

ARY: Which is a Prince song. Right. I mean, we know that the original is a Prince song. If you ain't never heard of it, please do listen to it. We've known it was a Prince song because house heads played Prince's "I Feel for You." The point that I'm making is that the Chaka Khan song is the basis of most of R and B today.

And when you think about that song, you had a rapper, which had not been done before in a pop song, a sampling of Stevie Wonder's "Fingertips," which had not been done, and him playing the harmonica. And although the "Chaka, Chaka Khan," being repeated in the song "I Feel For You" was originally a mistake that is made in the studio, it is reflective of the scratching that happens in what we know to be hip-hop, because it all has now been cultivated in hip-hop. Are you going to have a conversation about that?

MLH: That was my very next question. Keep on rolling, baby. Number four, can you talk about the intersections between house music and hip-hop in Chicago?

ARY: Here we go. So, there ain't hip-hop without the breakbeat, which is house music. I know hip-hop purists may argue that by saying, "No, the breakbeat is more progressive than house arrangements." But you have to understand, that percussion, or the percussive qualities of the breakbeat, is designed to get people to move, which is what the fuck house music is designed to do. The intention behind all of that is for people to move.

There will be no hip-hop music if hip-hop music was about a motherfucka sitting down and listening to motherfuckas talk. There will be no hip-hop music. Motherfuckas wouldn't been into it. That's a speakeasy over congas.

Saying, "Put your hands in the air, and wave 'em like you just don't care" is a call that requires a body to respond, which is house music. Think about it.

MLH: Even when you think about the history of hip-hop—Kool Herc's parties were community parties to make people's kids safe, and they were dancing to what we would call house music.

ARY: That's just the thing. I think people again allow adjectives and qualifiers to separate things. I do believe that there is an intentional homophobia in hip-hop. "If the disco is for the faggots, hip-hop has gotta be for the real 'real niggas.'"

MLH: Even though the "faggots and the real niggas" are the same person.

ARY: The gag is "real faggots are real niggas and vice versa, real niggas are real faggots." The real facts. Y'all all, kids, trust and believe. You're doing kid antics all the time. All the time. All the time.

But again, that is used to divide it, or to distinguish it, from what would be house, because you have to ask, you have to talk sexuality.

There are girls, girls and women, shaking their booties, coming to being somewhere, dressed to the pleasure of a cis-hetero male. She's an accessory, not necessity. See, that's the difference. A woman is a necessity in house, she's an accessory in hip-hop, which is a very dangerous place to put a Black woman's body. She ain't nothing but a bed wench at that point. There's a danger in that.

So over here, where she is and should be regarded as necessity, it's because a lot of what she is doing is being reimagined in the bodies of others. And I mean that more specifically, with queer folk. The queer boys want to be the doll. They want to be Josephine Baker. That's a Black woman's body. They then immolate that level of chicness, grandness, uninhabited movement.

MLH: Fabulosity.

ARY: Fabulosity. That's Black Girl Magic. All day long. The Big Mama Thorntons, the Bessie Smiths. There is queerness in that because they were queer people.

But the important thing about what I'm talking about, in terms of the Black woman as necessity in house music, is because Black women possess a body that a lot of folks don't.

When Mahalia Jackson is first singin' in churches and traveling and touring in churches, she is performing in a dress, a blouse, a skirt, whatever you come dressed in church with.

Mahalia Jackson is a voluptuous woman—breasts, hips, thighs.

She's singing and she is the spirit. She's moving and her body is moving kinda lapse. She's here, her titties are still there. And so they started dressing her in robes, because her body was enticing the deacons and that was sinful. She's moving, but she's bucking in the spirit of Jesus. It ain't to entice anybody, but it's enticing.

Here's where I get back to necessity. That body is doing a thing in house music that's not necessarily in the intent of enticing. In hip-hop, that's exactly what we take these titties and that booty to do. They feel like this door fee has now granted them access to the body that don't belong to them.

Here's where you get to talking about the problems of gender in this joint, and how they manifest in the context of hip-hop, and the context of how house music, and all of that is under the brink of patriarchy and misogyny. Then in hip-hop, queerness becomes a problem.

Because this ain't free love here. If I don't want you on my arm 'cause I don't get down like that, ain't no need for you over here.

MLH: Right, or ain't no need for you over here because somebody might find out my T.

ARY: Oh, you want to have that conversation.

MLH: Well, we got to have that conversation, 'cause they were the same motherfuckas.

ARY: Because we all understand that those gents over there ain't nothing but repackaged gents and girls from over here. Those of us who walk with a number of modifiers and adjectives, we know what we are looking at, every rip. Okay. And some of us have been at the hip-hop party because we been "with" motherfuckas at the hip-hop party. You know what I'm saying?

MLH: Right, right.

ARY: And we, some of us, have agreed to closet ourselves over at the hip-hop party because, again, over here at the house party, you don't have to do that. There's still dangers—people will say, "Well, that don't matter." That's a dangerous thing to say too, because all of me matters.

My work is to be my whole self in any room I enter. My goal ain't to be, "Oh, I can be this part of me at church, but I can't be this part of me at church." My argument is, well, if I can't be all of me at the church, why go to that church? When this space, where I can be everything I am, is church too. It's church too. This space that I just left to go to church, to go to the tabernacle—this house party, that warehouse I just left to go to the church house—is more accepting and safer, respectful, and honorable to all of my adjectives than this church house. So I argue that I cannot be in a church house if it doesn't honor all me and edify my spirit and be a place that is community. It can't be. It cannot be. It cannot be church.

Or at least a space in which I have to engage.

MLH: Damn. Thank you so much, Avery.

CONCLUSION

Nothing feels as good as a house music set. A slow, sinful, sultry sequence, a hot, funky jack joint, a down-tempo diva vocal, remixed. Sometimes during the break in the beat, they speak some wisdom or plead for late-night love, it all gets you there. As my friend Johnie Williams says, "You gotta find the groove and ride it." Whatever mood you're in, house music has no boundaries. What's considered a house song is limitless. If it's played at a house music party and people are dancing to it, then it's a house song.

In the nearly forty years since house music was born on the South Side of Chicago, so much has changed. You can go online and find a house party any day of the week, somewhere. (Though the word-of-mouth parties are still the most fire.) Now we can download mixes and listen to them on the cell phones in our pockets. DJs have become rock stars, and house, EDM, and dance music festivals draw crowds in the hundreds of thousands. There are so many genres of house music, it is almost impossible to count.

Chicago house music has helped shape dance music culture worldwide. People all around the world have love for Chicago because of house music (and President Obama, and Michael Jordan). It belongs to the world now, and in some ways, it always has. From its African roots, it has returned to the motherland and back, sprouting Afro-house through artists like Black Coffee, Kususa, Osunlade, and Saint Evo. I've heard Chicago-style house music in Sydney, Australia, where SASH hosts a weekly Sunday party, "By Day," that goes from 2:00 p.m. to 10:00 p.m., and "By Night" that goes from 11:00 p.m. until 11:00 a.m. the next morning, at a venue overlooking the Sydney Harbor (and they serve brunch). I've heard Chicago house in Auckland, New Zealand, in São Paulo and Salvador de Bahia, Brazil, in Colombo, Sri Lanka, and in Goa, India; from crowded torchlit beaches to exclusive moon-drenched rooftops. While the vibe and the decor are as different as the people, one thing remains the same—the feeling of the music and the expressions of love and togetherness. House music was given its name by the community, and no matter where you go, when there is house music playing, you will feel welcome, and you will make friends.

As of June 2023, the Warehouse, located at 206 South Jefferson has been given landmark status from the Commission on Chicago Landmarks. This sacred space will now be preserved for future generations.

Understanding the roots of Chicago house music is important because so much of Black culture and music has been co-opted by others. Chicago house music is a Black aesthetic, created and curated by Black people. And while we have shared our music and our culture with the world, Black blood, sweat, and tears literally went into the making of this music, this culture, these communities.

One of the golden ages of Chicago house music was the nineties. It was also the most devastating. We lost Ron Hardy. His passing left a hole in our hearts that has never quite been filled.

Many of our brothers and sisters lost their lives to drugs and drug use, random violence, and complications due to HIV/AIDS. Whole core groups of people died as the Black and Latinx communities tried to break free of stigma and denial. The people in the house community were some of the first to come together to provide food, comfort, safety, and shelter, and to raise money for the awareness and the culturally specific education that helped save lives and bring love to people affected with and impacted by HIV/AIDS, people in our communities who'd been living in shame, fear, and isolation. We were the ones who helped the Black and Latinx communities see that we could overcome and survive.

In the news, we often hear about the violence in Chicago, and a lot of it is true. But one of the places (and there are many) where you will always find peace—without prejudice or hate—is at a house music function. We take our house music seriously, and we hold its principles close to our hearts. All of us who come together in acceptance, love, peace, community, and freedom, under the banner of house music, we are all Guardians of the Flame.

References

INTRODUCTION

Marguerite Harrold, "Growing Up in Chicago House Music," *Chicago Review* 62:04/63:01/2: The Black Arts Movement in Chicago (Summer/Fall 2019). Ed. Andrew Peart, Eric Powell, and Gerónimo Sarmiento Cruz, www.chicagoreview.org/marguerite-l-harrold-growing-up-in-chicago-house-music.

CHAPTER 1: ROOTS AND ORIGINS

"A Condensed History of Chicago House Music, *Chicago* magazine (August 27, 2018), www.chicagomag.com/chicago-magazine/august-2018/house-music/a-condensed-history-of-chicago-house.

Patricia Hill Collins, *Black Feminist Thought: Knowledge, Consciousness, and the Politics of Empowerment* (Routledge, 2000).

Tilford Brooks, *America's Black Musical Heritage* (Pearson, 1984).

Ted Gioia, *Work Songs* (Duke University Press, 2006) and *Healing Songs* (Duke University Press, 2006).

Dakota A. Pippins, *The Jazz History Tree*, www.jazzhistorytree.com.

"A Timeline of Disco," *The Hoya*, thehoya.com/wp-content/uploads/2021/05/Disco-Timeline-Website.png.

"History of the Cylinder Phonograph," Library of Congress, www.loc.gov/collections/edison-company-motion-pictures-and-sound-recordings/articles-and-essays/history-of-edison-sound-recordings/history-of-the-cylinder-phonograph.

Hugh Schofield, "No Holding Back French Disco Diva," *BBC News* (October 24, 2005), news.bbc.co.uk/2/hi/europe/4372150.stm.

Robert D. McFadden, "Régine, Whose Discotheque Gave Nightlife a New Dawn, Dies at 92," May 1, 2022, *New York Times,* www.nytimes.com/2022/05/01/arts/regine-dead.html.

The Jim Crow Museum, "What Was Jim Crow," Ferris State University, www.ferris.edu/HTMLS/news/jimcrow/what.htm.

Sarah Pruitt, "What Happened at the Stonewall Riots? A Timeline of the 1969 Uprising," History.com, www.history.com/news/stonewall-riots-timeline.

CHAPTER 2: THE PIONEERS, 1970–1975

David Mancuso, "New York Stories: David Mancuso," *Red Bull Music Academy*, daily.redbullmusicacademy.com/2013/05/new-york-stories-david-mancuso.

Bill Brewster and Frank Broughton, "Interview: David Mancuso," *Red Bull Music Academy*, November 15, 2016, daily.redbullmusicacademy.com/2016/11/david-mancuso-dj-history-interview.

Otis Alexander, "Soul Train (1970–2006)," *Black Past*, www.blackpast.org/african-american-history/soul-train-1970-2006.

"Nicky Siano on the Gallery, Larry Levan, and Life after Music," Red Bull Music Academy, www.youtube.com/watch?v=KR6pHVkzuew.

Nohashi Records, "Larry Levan Interview & Live @ Mars June 6, 1990," www.youtube.com/watch?v=zzWhTNvw9qA.

Rory PQ, "Hip Hop History: From the Streets to the Mainstream," *Icon Collective*, November 13, 2019, iconcollective.edu/hip-hop-history.

The phrase "Racing against the Ultimate Wackness" is a line from the Netflix series, *The Get Down*, created by Stephen Adly Guirgis and Baz Luhrmann.

Discoguy, "Sharon White," *disco-disco.com*, www.disco-disco.com/djs/sharon.shtml.

CHAPTER 3: THE ORIGINATORS, 1976–1989

Robert Williams, "The Birth of House Music," *Chicago* magazine, August 27, 2018, www.chicagomag.com/chicago-magazine/august-2018/house-music/the-birth-of-house.

Czarina Mirani, "Who is Robert Williams?" *5Mag.net*, December 1, 2005, 5mag.net/features/who-is-robert-williams.

"Frankie Knuckles on the Birth of House Music," *Red Bull Music Academy,* daily.redbullmusicacademy.com/2018/02/frankie-knuckles-1995-interview.

Jeff "Chairman" Mao, interview with Frankie Knuckles, *Red Bull Music Academy,* www.redbullmusicacademy.com/lectures/frankie-knuckles-lecture.

"Ron Hardy, Biography," *Resident Advisor*, 2023, ra.co/dj/ronhardy/biography.

Jacob Arnold, "Ron Hardy at the Music Box," *Red Bull Music Academy*, May 18, 2015, daily.redbullmusicacademy.com/2015/05/ron-hardy-at-the-music-box.

"Herb Kent," *The History Makers: The Digital Repository for the Black Experience*, www.thehistorymakers.org/biography/herb-kent-39.

"Vera Washington & Pat McCombs," *Chicago Gay History*, www.chicagogayhistory.com/biography.php?id=633.

"Lori Branch," *LoriBranch.com* www.lorabranch.com.

DJ Celeste Alexander (@celestethedj), Instagram, www.instagram.com/celestethedj.

Go Bang Mag, "Toni Shelton / Another Toni Shelton Production," July 1, 2020, gobangmagazine.com/2020/07/01/business-music-nightlife-toni-shelton-another-toni-shelton-production.

"WBMX and the Hot Mix 5," *The Beat Chicago*, thebeatchicago.com/wbmx-hot-mix-5-retrospective.

Steve Johnson, "Revamp Planned for Juice Bar Law," *Chicago Tribune*, January 7, 1987, www.chicagotribune.com/news/ct-xpm-1987-01-07-8701020675-story.html.

CHAPTER 4: THE INNOVATORS, 1990–2000

3 Degrees Global, Facebook, www.facebook.com/3degreesglobal.

"3 Degrees Global," *Resident Advisor*, 2023, ra.co/promoters/2730.

Michael Gebert, "Freshly Made Food Comes to Englewood at the Dream Café & Grille," *Fooditor*, fooditor.com/freshly-made-food-comes-englewood-dream-cafe-grille.

"David Risqué," *Mapping Arts Project, Chicago*, 2023, mappingartsproject.org/chicago/artists/david-risque.

Terry Matthew, "Superjane at 20," *5Mag.net*, 5mag.net/features/superjane-at-20.

Colette (@djcolette), Instagram, www.instagram.com/djcolette.

Djheather, Facebook, www.facebook.com/djheatherchicago.

DJ Heather (@djheather), Instagram, www.instagram.com/djheather.
"DJ Heather," *Insomniac*, www.insomniac.com/music/artists/dj-heather.
Jan Hiegellke, "Music 45: Who Rocks Chicago's Music World 2008," *New City Music*, music.newcity.com/2008/05/08/music-45-who-rocks-chicagos-music-world-2008.
"About," *DJ Lady D*, www.djladydchicago.com/about-1.
Rachel Kupfer, "Honor the Birth of House Music with 10 Influential Black Artists from Chicago," *edm.com*, edm.com/features/black-history-month-10-influential-black-artists-from-chicago.
Czarina Mirani, "3 Degrees Global Spotlight Volume 1—mixed by bigSEXY," April 10, 2014, 5mag.net/audio/3-degrees-global-bigsexy-mix.

CHAPTER 5: GUARDIANS OF THE FLAME, 2000–PRESENT

"How the Silver Room Founder Eric Williams is Keeping Chicago Connected to the Digital Era," *Do 312*, do312.com/p/on-the-rise-chicago-feat-eric-williams-of-the-silver-room.
"Biography, Czboogie," *Resident Advisor*, 2023, ra.co/dj/czboogie/biography.
Salem Collo-Julin, "Interview with Mario Smith," *Chicago Reader*, November 10, 2022, chicagoreader.com/people-issue/2022-11-10/mario-smith.

CONCLUSION

"The Warehouse, Birthplace of House Music, Takes Key Step Toward Becoming a Chicago Landmark." *Block Club Chicago*, April 13, 2023, blockclubchicago.org/2023/04/13/the-warehouse-birthplace-of-house-music-takes-first-key-step-toward-becoming-a-chicago-landmark.

About the Author

Marguerite L. Harrold is a poet, teacher, environmentalist, and community activist from Chicago. She has a master of fine arts in creative writing from Columbia College Chicago. Her work has been featured in anthologies, including *The Spaces Between Us: Poetry, Prose and Art on HIV/AIDS; Anthology House: A Visionary Ecology Project*; and *The Book of Bad Betties*. Her poems and essays have appeared in *Obsidian, Chicago Review, jubilat, Anti-Heroin Chic, RHINO, Vinyl Poetry and Prose,* and other literary journals. She is a member of the Community of Writers, an alumna of the Bread Loaf Orion Environmental Writer's Conference, and a 2021/2022 Hugo House Fellow. She is an associate editor of *Prairie Schooner* and the educational promotions manager for the African Poetry Book Fund.